04/23

STRAND PRICE

FOR $5.00 EACH

D0810346

Praise for

Facing the Fire

"Chief Cochran is an example of the character and the cost required of those who choose to live for something beyond themselves, especially in an age where nearly every voice tells us to live for our own happiness. He has that character, forged through years of hard work and commitment to God, and he's experienced the cost of choosing obedience over comfort, believing that Christ would be present in his fiery trial. I thank God that this story is now available to the world in this book."

—**John Stonestreet,** president of the Colson Center and host of *BreakPoint*

"This true story will give you strength. Kelvin Cochran is a terrific storyteller, and in this memoir he describes the experiences that forged his character. If you're interested in learning how a hero is made, this is the book for you."

—**Eric Metaxas,** #1 *New York Times* bestselling author and host of the nationally syndicated *Eric Metaxas Radio Show*

"Kelvin Cochran is a hero and a fighter. This beautifully written book tells his story of not only fighting fires but overcoming his childhood poverty to then fight racial discrimination because of the color of his skin and religious discrimination because of his Christian beliefs. All along he demonstrates what faithful discipleship entails. Chief Cochran is an inspirational witness to truths of human sexuality, racial equality, and religious liberty."

—**Ryan T. Anderson, Ph.D.,** president of the Ethics and Public Policy Center and author of *Truth Overruled: The Future of Marriage and Religious Freedom* and *When Harry Became Sally: Responding to the Transgender Moment*

"*Facing the Fire* is a must-read, particularly for those surmounting circumstances which challenge our faith. I've had a front-row seat watching Dr. Cochran maintain his integrity while facing adversity with courage and discipline. His journey of unwavering faith is an inspirational testament for us all as we face the fires that forge our faith."

    —Dr. Craig L. Oliver Sr., senior pastor of Elizabeth Baptist Church in Atlanta, Georgia

Facing the Fire

Facing the Fire

The Faith That Brought
"America's Fire Chief" through the
Flames of Persecution

Kelvin J. Cochran
with Andy Butcher

SALEM
BOOKS
an imprint of Regnery Publishing
Washington, D.C.

Copyright © 2021 by Kelvin J. Cochran

All rights reserved. No part of this publication may be reproduced or transmitted in any form or by any means electronic or mechanical, including photocopy, recording, or any information storage and retrieval system now known or to be invented, without permission in writing from the publisher, except by a reviewer who wishes to quote brief passages in connection with a review written for inclusion in a magazine, newspaper, website, or broadcast.

All Scripture quotations, unless otherwise indicated, are taken from the Holy Bible, New International Version®, NIV®. Copyright © 1973, 1978, 1984, 2011 by Biblica, Inc.™ Used by permission of Zondervan. All rights reserved worldwide. www.zondervan.com. The "NIV" and "New International Version" are trademarks registered in the United States Patent and Trademark Office by Biblica, Inc.™

Scriptures marked BSB are taken from the The Holy Bible, Berean Study Bible, BSB. Copyright © 2016, 2018 by Bible Hub. Used by permission. All rights reserved worldwide.

Scriptures marked KJV are taken from the KING JAMES VERSION, public domain.

Scriptures marked NASB are taken from the NEW AMERICAN STANDARD BIBLE®. Copyright © 1960, 1962, 1963, 1968, 1971, 1972, 1973, 1975, 1977, 1995 by the Lockman Foundation. Used by permission.

Scriptures marked NKJV are taken from the NEW KING JAMES VERSION.® Copyright © 1982 by Thomas Nelson, Inc. Used by permission. All rights reserved.

Scriptures marked NLT are taken from the HOLY BIBLE, NEW LIVING TRANSLATION. Copyright © 1996, 2004, 2007 by Tyndale House Foundation. Used by permission of Tyndale House Publishers, Inc., Carol Stream, Illinois, 60188. All rights reserved.

Published in association with the literary agency of Legacy, LLC, 501 N. Orlando Avenue, Suite #313–348, Winter Park, FL 32789.

Salem Books™ is a trademark of Salem Communications Holding Corporation

Regnery® is a registered trademark and its colophon is a trademark of Salem Communications Holding Corporation

Cataloging-in-Publication data on file with the Library of Congress

ISBN: 978-1-68451-161-7
eISBN: 978-1-68451-210-2

Library of Congress Control Number: 2020951630

Published in the United States by
Salem Books
An Imprint of Regnery Publishing
A Division of Salem Media Group
Washington, D.C.
www.SalemBooks.com

Manufactured in the United States of America

10 9 8 7 6 5 4 3 2 1

Books are available in quantity for promotional or premium use. For information on discounts and terms, please visit our website: www.SalemBooks.com.

This book is dedicated to my wife, Carolyn;
our children: Tiffane, Kelton, and Camille;
and our granddaughter, Thailynn.

Without your love and support,
I would not have a story to tell.

CONTENTS

CHAPTER ONE

Caught in the Flames

When you walk through the fire, you will not be
burned; the flames will not set you ablaze.

—Isaiah 43:2

Hollywood familiarized the world with one of the deadliest threats a firefighter can face through the 1991 action movie *Backdraft*. It took its name from the explosion that occurs when fierce flames that have consumed all the surrounding oxygen suddenly find a new source—maybe when someone unaware of the danger opens a door, or when the intense heat shatters a window. The result is a deadly fireball.

More common, though, and equally dangerous is a flashover. This too is a sudden and catastrophic explosion. The cause is very different, however. As a fire spreads in a contained space, it starts to heat everything there. In just a short time, whatever is in the room will begin to give off gases—furniture, books, clothing, you name it. At some point, somewhere around 1,100 degrees Fahrenheit—the temperature of the glowing lava spewed from an active volcano—all those gases are ignited in a big boom. Caught in the flames, nothing survives. I had been a firefighter for just a couple of years when I experienced my first flashover. If not for being in just the right place at that moment and the hours of training that had taught me how to respond, it could have ended my life that October night in 1983.

Some thirty years later, the same kind of positioning and preparation would see me through a different kind of flashover—a spiritual one that consumed my career.

■　　■　　■

As a twenty-three-year-old rookie, I was excited when the alarm sounded sometime after midnight at Station Nine in Shreveport, Louisiana. I knew it signaled that someone might be in danger somewhere, and I didn't take any pleasure from that. But it also meant I had the opportunity to help someone in crisis, and that was a passion I had carried since I was a small boy watching firefighters tackle a blaze at a neighbor's house.

Shaking off the fog of sleep, I sat up in my bed and turned to step into the bunker-gear pants left ready for easy access. I pulled them up, looping my arms through the shoulder straps. After sliding down the firehouse pole, I climbed into the back of Rescue Truck Number Two with the rest of my crew as I finished dressing.

I considered the rescue truck a prime spot. Smaller than the other engines, it didn't have hoses and water. Instead, it was equipped with all kinds of rescue gear: extrication tools, emergency medical equipment, and splints. Our job was to dive in and save whoever and whatever we could. There was no official "elite" classification, but that was how many firefighters viewed the assignment. I loved being one of those selected for the position.

The call-out over the loudspeaker had alerted us to a "working fire" in the Southern Hills area. Like cab drivers, firefighters get to know a city pretty well over time. I had been at Station Nine long enough to know that we were going to one of the nicest areas of Shreveport, which was much more desirable than the area where I'd grown up.

We arrived at a single-story assembly hall on Meriwether Road, which was used by a church on Sunday mornings and as a community meeting place the rest of the week. The fire was visible at the rear of the building, where it seemed to have taken a strong hold. Along with Don, with whom I had graduated from the city's firefighter academy a couple of years previously, I was instructed to go into the empty building from the front and see if we could attack the flames from inside.

With all our gear and self-contained breathing apparatuses, we were each wearing about fifty pounds, but we weren't weighed down. We were young and in the best shape of our lives. We had practiced and practiced and practiced while wearing all our equipment so often that, in time, we felt no more restricted in our mobility by all the cumbersome gear than if we had been wearing pajamas. Carrying a hose, we crawled in through the front door on our hands and knees. The seat of the fire may have been in the back, but it was already making its presence felt. The large, open meeting room was hot and filled with heavy black smoke. We had to get down where it was cooler and visibility was a little better.

Nosing our way carefully past rows of chairs, we found the right-hand wall, a firefighter's Lesson Number One in safety. When you go into a dark room, you always locate the wall to the left or the right and then stay with it until you find your way to where you need to go. That way, if you need to get out, you just have to turn around and trace your way back the way you came with the wall on your opposite hand. It's like a tactile version of a breadcrumb trail. When it's hot and dark and dangerous, it's easy to get disoriented very quickly, even if you know your whereabouts well. Danger messes with your sense of direction, so you have to be able to get out without having to think too much about it.

Don and I checked in on each other through our voice boxes as we maneuvered down the wall. From time to time the captain would break in over our radios, asking for a progress report. We were about halfway down the wall toward the rear of the building when there was a loud crackling sound, fierce above the other muffled fire noises. Before we had the chance to do anything, the ceiling above us collapsed in a cloud of flame, burning debris, and smoke. All we could do was hit the ground flat and hope for the best.

No one was aware that the fire had spread up from the rear of the building into the loft space that ran across the whole of the structure. Like a giant oven, the enclosed space had gotten hotter and hotter until all the beams and the insulation and whatever had been stored up there had begun to give off gas and suddenly reach its ignition point—a flashover.

If Don and I had been up there, that would have been the end of us. As it was, we were incredibly fortunate. As the ceiling collapsed, it could have dropped straight down and trapped or even crushed us. Instead, it came down in the center of the room, with the beams falling at such an angle that they formed a small "V," a safe void space between the floor and wall, in which we now lay. The heat was now even more intense, and there was burning debris all around us.

"Don, you okay?" I asked.

"Yeah," he answered. "You, Klein?" I'd been given the nickname—every new firefighter gets one—because the guys said my name reminded them of the fashion designer Calvin Klein.

"Yep," I said. "Let's get out of here."

The small crawlspace that had been created by the collapse wasn't wide or high enough for us to turn around, so we wiggled our way out backward. As we did, the captain's voice came over the radio, wanting to know if we were okay and telling us to come on out straight away. We were happy to follow orders.

We weren't back out at the front of the building very long before it all collapsed behind us with a loud *whoomph*! Strange as it may sound, my heart wasn't beating too fast. I had enough respect for fire to know it could have ended badly for Don and me. But we hadn't taken any unnecessary risks; there is a difference between being cavalier and being courageous, and I also trusted our training. I knew we had been prepared for the worst. All we had practiced and rehearsed had kicked in right when we needed it.

■　　　■　　　■

So many lessons in my firefighting career have been transferable to my spiritual journey. The same kind of faith in what I

had learned that saw me through a near-miss as a young firefighter would prove to be my salvation and protection over thirty
years later upon my termination. This time the flashover didn't
bring down a roof; it brought down my career—one which had
seen me achieve more than I ever could have imagined.

Standing on the shoulders of others who had challenged the
predominantly white-male culture of the Shreveport Fire
Department, my service had not only helped to further dis-
mantle the historic racism there, but by the grace of God I
advanced through the ranks to become the city's first black fire
chief. It was a proud appointment. If I had served the entirety
of my fire service in Shreveport, I would have been more than
satisfied, but God had greater plans: the honor of leading a fire
department in one of America's most dynamic cities, Atlanta,
and a season serving under President Barack Obama as the
United States fire administrator—the highest fire service post in
the nation.

Flashovers, whether physical or spiritual, may appear to happen all of a sudden, but they are actually the final step in a series
of events that take place before a house becomes fully engulfed in
flames. By sifting through the charred remains once a fire is out,
investigators may be able to trace it back to a first single spark. I
discovered that in some ways, you might say I had actually caused
the spark of what became my career-burning flashover, though I
was not aware of it at the time.

Ironically enough, it was because I was trying to provide
some illumination—"letting my light shine" before others. I
knew the success I had enjoyed in my career wasn't just because
of my own talents and efforts, though I had certainly always tried

to do the best I could. No, the achievements and accolades I had experienced and received were blessings from God as I did my best to walk in His ways. Faith had guided me from poverty and a broken home to financial security, emotional wholeness, and a loving family. Having experienced workplace prejudice first-hand, I also had done what I could to ensure that others did not experience the same thing, for any reason—be it their ethnicity, their religion, or their sexual identity.

Not that I had done everything right all the time. There had been bumps along the way, no question—times when I had failed to live up to God's standards. But through it all He had been faithful, and now after many years of following Christ, I wanted other men to know they had access to the same hope for a better life as I did.

■   ■   ■

My experience from being in church over the years was that too few Christian men wholeheartedly believed we were transformed from sinners to the righteousness of God in Christ. Yes, they believed in God, and yes, they believed that He loved them and had forgiven their sins through Jesus's death and resurrection. But somehow that didn't seem to permeate to the very core of their being—present company included. Many of the men I interacted with at church seemed to still carry the weight of guilt from the shortcomings of their past. They struggled with shame over ways and habits that made the pursuit of godliness seem like an exercise in futility, leaving them feeling like they never could be all that God wanted them to be.

This did not line up with the truth I'd come to know by that point in my walk of faith. By dying on the cross and rising from the dead, Jesus defeated sin and death once and for all. That is why in Romans 8:1 the Apostle Paul wrote, "So now there is no condemnation for those who belong to Christ Jesus." Not some condemnation, depending on how "good" you are. None! And yet so many men I knew did not seem to be living in the light of that reality.

While facilitating a men's small group study at my church, I became intrigued by the question God asked Adam in Genesis 3:11: "Who told you that you were naked?" It occurred to me that maybe God wasn't just asking Adam how he had learned he didn't have any clothes on. I began to do some research, following what seemed to be a trail God had laid out that kept leading me deeper and deeper into His Word.

The result was what I believed to be an important message for so many Christian men: that the nakedness God was speaking about was more than just physical. He was alluding to the loss of the spiritual "clothing" of God's glory that Adam had when he was created, and which he forfeited when he sinned. The lamb God slaughtered to clothe Adam was a precursor to the Lamb of God—Jesus Christ—who would come to take away the sins of the whole world. Those who are baptized in Christ are now clothed with Him, according to Galatians 3:27. Covered in Christ, we are freed from guilt and shame and condemnation. We can live as the men we were created to be—in our families, in our communities, and in our workplaces.

So I wrote a short book about that topic and decided to make it available to anyone who might find help in its pages.

Though I titled my book *Who Told You That You Were Naked?*, it wasn't about sex. In fact, that topic occupied only a handful of the book's 162 pages. I addressed the issue briefly from a biblical perspective, but mostly I explored what it looked like for men to understand and live in the freedom God offers through a relationship with Jesus.

I self-published the book in November 2013, never expecting it to be a big seller. I simply wanted to put what I had discovered through my studies into a form that would be accessible for others. As part of the process of preparing it for publication, I contacted the city of Atlanta's ethics officer. I wanted to make sure there would be no problems with my writing a faith-based book on my own time and mentioning in the bio that I was the Atlanta fire chief. The ethics officer told me there would be no problem with my doing that as long as the book was not about city government or the fire department (which it wasn't). She even asked me to give her a copy when it came out.

Upon completion, I sold a handful of copies to guys in my church back in Shreveport and gave away a few to people I thought might be interested. In March 2014, I took three copies along with me to the mayor's annual State of the City Breakfast downtown and gave two council members whom I knew to be Christians one copy apiece. Understanding Atlanta Mayor Kasim Reed to be a man of faith—he'd once joined me in a fast I did—I had already dropped off a personally inscribed copy for him with his executive assistant. I also passed along copies to a few people in the department whom I knew well—guys who were Christians like me.

■   ■   ■

A year later, I had pretty much forgotten about all that when I got a call at my office at the Public Safety Headquarters one day in November 2014. It was from someone I knew who worked in the constituent services department over at City Hall.

That person warned me to be on guard at the annual Breakfast With Our Bravest event, which was scheduled for the following morning. Some of the media might be there with some questions, she told me, because a council member who had received a copy of my book twelve months earlier was offended by its contents. I thanked my caller for the heads-up and said I would be prepared for the next day...but when I hung up, I quickly put it all out of my mind.

That may have stemmed in part from my years as a firefighter: when faced with a difficult situation, you learn not to react reflexively but to slow down. But mostly it was because I knew I hadn't written anything that should give rise to any concern. My reaction, or lack of it, seemed justified when the awards breakfast honoring exemplary service went off the following day without incident.

But over the next few days, I received a couple more calls from people I knew in the administration who wanted to tip me off about a possible storm brewing over the book. Once again, I thanked them, but I still didn't put much stock in what they were saying.

Over the weekend, I called Mayor Reed's office. I wasn't worried about what might have been coming, but I wanted some advice from his communications team on the best way to respond if any media did contact me. I'd been part of city government leadership long enough to know that things could quickly get out of hand if they weren't handled properly. It was important that the city administration speak with a unified voice, and I assumed we all wanted to make it clear that there really wasn't any issue with the book or what I had written.

On November 24—a Monday morning—I attended the funeral of a retired firefighter. While traveling to the church, I tried again to reach the mayor's office. With no success there, I also called the city's chief operating officer. He was unavailable as well. Then I got a call from the city's human resources director, who asked me to report to her office after the service.

My internal fire alarm finally started ringing when I got there. I was greeted by the human resources director, the mayor's chief of staff, and one of the city's attorneys. A copy of my book lay on the desk. The heat began to rise significantly in the very businesslike room, as though it were filling with smoke. They told me parts of the book were "problematic": the fact that I identified myself as the fire chief of Atlanta, that I wrote about having the responsibility to care for and cultivate the fire department "to the glory of God", and that the parts where I quoted the Bible's teaching on human sexuality were offensive to the LGBT community. All these allegations were like flammable gases being released into the now super-heated atmosphere.

The group told me that Mayor Reed didn't support my position and that I was going to be suspended without pay for thirty days. That was when it hit me: flashover! I was caught in the flames.

During my suspension, I was told, the city would conduct a thorough investigation. After that time, I would have to complete some sensitivity training before I could resume my duties. They did not want me talking to the media while I was suspended.

I sat quietly as they explained all this to me. Then I told them I understood the political nature of the issue and how the mayor had to do this; I got it. Privately, I was thinking that an investigation would prove there was no basis for a complaint against me. With no evidence, the city would restore my losses and return me to my post.

The meeting ended cordially enough as I made one request: I wanted the city to inform the media on my behalf that I would not be able to do any interviews during my suspension, should I be approached. They said they would do that for me.

The suspension began immediately. I drove from the meeting straight to my office, where I picked up a few items, and then headed home. On the way, I began receiving calls from friends, telling me they had heard about the city's action on the news. Already? I was shocked; I thought the administration had intended to keep things under wraps as best as possible.

It turned out that they only wanted *me* to be silent. At the same time that I was learning about my suspension in that meeting with the three representatives, I later discovered, it was being announced from another part of City Hall. The city was pitching the story the way it wanted it to be read: that I was in the wrong. And I had agreed to remain quiet, unable to give my side.

I knew that people would be making judgments about me from what limited information they were given, but I wasn't dismayed. "God, I trust You completely," I told Him. I was confident that, while what had happened might have caught me off guard, God was not caught off guard. He knew exactly what was going on. Not only that, but He had already been preparing me for what I was facing. As David declared in Psalm 23, goodness and mercy had been following me all the days of my life, even though I had not been aware of it at all times.

"This is in Your hands," I told God. "I realize this is an opportunity for me to show my hope and trust in You, to demonstrate all that You have poured into me. People are going to be watching for how a man of faith responds, and I want to represent You well."

Despite all that was going on, I felt remarkably calm. It was like that first flashover: the roof may have caved in, but God had protected me, and I would come out of this unscathed if I followed what I knew to do. I was down on my knees while facing the fire in the community hall, and I was going to stay on my knees through this firestorm.

God would prove faithful to His promise of Isaiah 43:2: "When you walk through the fire, you will not be burned; the flames will not set you ablaze."

CHAPTER TWO

A Dream Ignited

*All the days ordained for me were written in your book
before one of them came to be.*

—*Psalm 139:16*

Many boys go through a phase of wanting to be a firefighter when they grow up, but typically the dream fades as time goes by. But I was captivated by the idea when I was five years old and never really wavered. It was a flame that never went out. Fire needs three things to burn—heat, fuel, and oxygen—and my passion was the same. Poverty was the fuel, faith was the oxygen, and the day Miss Mattie's house caught fire was the spark that lit everything.

The beginning of a fire is known as its incipient phase. The incipient phase of my firefighting dream can be traced back to one Sunday afternoon in 1965 as I lay on the floor of our cramped shotgun house with my five siblings while watching television. We had fairly good reception on our small black-and-white set, thanks to the coat hanger jammed in where the antenna should have been. It had been broken off long before—by accident or intent, I don't recall—and used as a sword when my brothers and I played Zorro.

I loved watching *The Andy Griffith Show* after our morning services at Galilee Baptist Church. Andy, Opie, Aunt Bea, and the others made me smile, but there was an element of sadness too. The sweet, safe, small-town life on the screen was something of a contrast to my environment. The show also made me yearn for my absent father.

My escape time in Mayberry was interrupted by the siren of a fire engine. Such alarms were commonplace in the neighborhood; the cheaply built, partially wooden homes caught fire easily. But this was not background noise from some blocks away—this seemed to be right outside. We ran to the front door and opened it. Sure enough, a large, bright-red fire truck was parked in front of Miss Mattie's place directly across the street. She was an older lady who lived alone and wasn't home at the time, so someone passing by must have spotted the flames and called the fire department. I could see the fire through the front porch window, black smoke escaping all around it. We stood, watching the crew go into action.

I was transfixed as the firefighters jumped off the truck, pulling on big black boots and tugging the hose off the side of the vehicle. I was struck by how calm and controlled they seemed in the middle of all the noise. A still center in the storm. My heart stirred when they entered the house to douse the flames. I could not get over how brave and caring they were to put themselves at risk to help someone else. They may have been wearing big helmets and heavy jackets rather than masks and tights, but I thought they were superheroes. And I wanted to be just like them.

I turned to my mom and siblings as we stood watching. "I want to be a fireman when I grow up," I declared.

Something lodged deep in my heart that day. From then on, whenever I would hear a fire engine, I would jump on my banana-seat bike and pedal off in the direction of the sound. I'd pull up near the scene and stand and watch the crews go into action.

There was a fire station close to the church we attended each Sunday, which I always enjoyed passing. When we moved to a new house close to the fire station on Garden Street, sometimes the big doors would be open, and I could catch a glimpse of the engines and the firemen at work inside. Occasionally, my friends and I would sneak in to snatch a mouthful of water from the drinking fountain in the station. I'd tell myself that maybe one day I'd be working there.

■　　■　　■

It wasn't just the firemen's bravery that captured my attention the day they came to put out the blaze at Miss Mattie's house. Though I was too young to really articulate it, part of me somehow recognized that these men were not only doing good for others; they were probably also doing pretty well for themselves. I figured that with such a worthwhile job, they likely weren't poor like my family was. And I certainly didn't like being poor.

Living in the projects indicated that you weren't doing well financially. So if you could no longer even afford to live in the projects, you were clearly in a serious situation. I first became aware of how tough things were when we had to leave our government-subsidized housing in Alameda Terrace in the Allendale area of the city.

I had been taken home there after arriving at Shreveport's Confederate Memorial Hospital on January 23, 1960. I was the fourth son born to George and Jane Cochran. Two sisters would follow, making for a large family to provide for through my parents' limited earnings. Neither of them went to college after high school; Dad worked for a grocery store, while Mom was employed by a dry cleaner. Money was tight enough without Dad's drinking—which, combined with his womanizing, brought their marriage to an end when I was three years old. Having married right out of high school, Mom was a single mother of six by the time she was thirty. With Dad no longer providing, she couldn't afford to stay in Alameda Terrace. We were evicted. We were "poor" when Dad was with us; after he left us, we became "po." We did not have enough income to qualify for the whole word "p-o-o-r."

That step down took us from the projects to a shotgun house, a three-room shack on Rear Snow Street. Adding the Rear to a street name identified it as the back alley, where the shotgun houses were of inferior quality compared to those on the main street. They were called "shotgun" because their in-a-line rooms meant that if all the doors were open, you could shoot a gun through the front door and the bullet would exit out the back without touching anything. These shotgun homes dated back to the early 1900s, originally built for white families who moved out to nicer neighborhoods as economic circumstances improved for them. By the time we moved into one, they were old, dilapidated rental properties predominantly found in black neighborhoods.

The floors were wooden and uneven. In some places, the floor covering was missing, and you could actually see through to the ground below and watch chickens fighting underneath the house or feed the neighborhood dogs that sniffed around for scraps. The roofs were made of corrugated tin sheets, which produced a distinctive drumming sound when it rained.

All six of us kids were squeezed into one bedroom. My three brothers and I shared the same bed. It wasn't much—an old box spring and an old mattress stacked up on some bricks, with boards across the top of them to hold everything in place. The two girls shared the relatively luxurious space (compared to us boys) of an old box spring and mattress the size of a twin bed held up by bricks and boards.

Even here, Mom's dry-cleaning wages were still not enough. Food stamps and welfare helped supplement her meager income, but there always seemed to be more month than money. That meant that we often didn't have use of all the utilities at the same time. Something was always off. There were times we would come home from school and flip the light switch, only to discover there was no electricity. Or I might pick up the phone to call Meme, our grandmother, and there would be no dial tone.

Other times the gas would be off, and we had to cook all our food on an electric plate until the bill was paid. There were even occasions when the water was turned off. Mom would tell us kids to fill all the empty milk jugs, bottles, and pots we could find. The first time this happened, I didn't understand why until a few days later, when I came home from school, turned on a faucet, and no water came out. Apparently, Mom had received a past-due notice and knew it would only be a matter of days before the water would be turned off. So we used the water we had collected to bathe, to cook with, and to flush the toilet until she could afford to have our account reinstated. One time when our supply ran out, we even had to ask for water from the neighbors.

I wasn't aware at the time how all this was like an exhausting game of chess for Mom, working out which move to make and which piece to temporarily sacrifice. The seasons had a lot to do with her strategic choices—summers meant it was lighter in the evenings, and there was less need for heat. No gas in the winter months meant cold nights, and no power during summer meant sitting in candlelight.

It wasn't uncommon for us to use up all the food stamps we were entitled to before the month was up. When that happened, Mom could scrape together just enough money to buy bread. We would have toast with Brer Rabbit syrup for breakfast and may-onnaise sandwiches for lunch and dinner. All the soda pops and Kool-Aid would be gone by that stage too, so if we wanted something sweet to drink, we'd stir a couple of teaspoons of sugar into a cold glass of water and have sugar water with our mayonnaise sandwiches.

As a kid, you think what you experience is normal until you start to compare your life with your friends' lives. I began to realize we were on a lower rung of the economic ladder than most folks around us when I found out that other families in the area, even in shotgun houses like ours, didn't have to juggle their utilities like we did. I also became aware that my friends would be slipped a few coins most Friday nights to go down to the corner store and buy some candy. For us, that was a rare treat.

We might not have had a lot, but we were expected to make the most of it. "We may be poor," Mama would tell us, "but we are not going to live in a filthy house." We didn't have any grass in our small yard, but she made us pick up any trash and rake the dirt so it looked smooth. My clothes were mostly hand-me-downs, but though they were well-worn, I had to keep them clean and tidy and be sure I was well turned out. Unlike many of the other kids, we didn't get new clothes at the start of each school year. Replacement pants and shirts came on an as-really-needed basis.

Despite her financial struggles, Mom always made Christmas really special somehow. We'd have a Christmas tree, and she managed to scrape together enough money to ensure that we got gifts. Then we would go over to Meme's for a feast.

Mom had a tough childhood of her own. The youngest and only girl among five kids, she was expected to help look after her brothers, who seemed to get preferential treatment. From what I can tell from Mom's stories, she was kind of a Cinderella figure in the home. By the time we came along, her mother had softened some. We loved visiting our grandmother at all times of the year. Meme always had milk and juice in the fridge, as well as little snacks—treats that we didn't get at home. Sometimes she would give Mom food when our pantry was really bare.

With all the financial pressures in mind, it's not surprising that Mom was tired most of the time. She was very loving, but she didn't have a lot of patience for what she considered to be nonsense. In particular, she expected us to treat adults with respect and to be kind to one another. As far as she was concerned, all we had was each other, so we couldn't be at odds. Her constant reminder was, "Charity begins at home and spreads abroad."

For the most part, we kids all got along pretty well. Especially when you consider we were in cramped conditions with little and sometimes no money. On the occasions when my older brothers would get into a fight, Mom would jump in and stamp it out in no uncertain terms. Her disciplinary style would definitely not be acceptable these days. If anyone ever got in trouble away from home, there would be serious consequences. "I'm whipping you now so the police won't be whipping you later," she'd declare.

Mom taught me the importance of honesty—and, unknowingly, that sometimes it can even be painful to tell the truth. If there was a troublemaker in the house, it was my second-oldest brother, Danny. He wasn't a bad kid, but he did like to stir things up when Mom wasn't around. One day when I was in seventh grade, I was walking to school when I stuck my hand into the pocket of my green windbreaker. It closed on something I could not identify; I pulled out my hand and—*whoa!*—a Mickey Mouse watch. I had no idea who it belonged to or how it had gotten into my jacket, but I decided to start wearing it.

Mom noticed my new timepiece a few days later. When she asked where it had come from, I told her that I didn't know; I had just found it in my pocket.

"You're lying to me," she said.

"No, ma'am, I'm not lying," I told her. "It was just in my jacket, so I started wearing it."

"Kelvin, you're lying to me. You'd better tell me the truth right now or I'm going to tear your butt up."

I desperately maintained my innocence, but she was having none of it. Mom got her belt and tanned my hide despite my protests. Then she asked me again.

"Honest, Mama, I don't know where it came from."

She gave me another whipping, and then a third when I continued to say I didn't know anything about where the watch had come from. "We're gonna keep this up until you tell me the truth, son," she said.

"Samuel," I told her quietly. Looking for some way out of Mom's crosshairs, I decided to blame it on my best friend. "Samuel gave it to me."

Unfortunately, this lie ended up only making things worse. Mom got on the phone to Samuel's mother, who in turn gave him a whipping. But his denials must have resonated with her, because when Mom ended the call, she gave me another thrashing for lying about Samuel.

"We're gonna keep this up all night if we have to," she told me.

By this time, I didn't know what was stinging more—my rear end or my heart. I just wanted it all to be over.

"I stole it," I finally said in a whisper.

That fake confession earned me yet one more licking with the belt, but then, at last, it was over.

Many years later, as we all sat around the table together one Thanksgiving reminiscing as adults, I ruefully recalled the Mickey Mouse Watch Inquisition. Only then did Danny confess that he had gotten the watch somehow and left it in my pocket when he had borrowed my jacket.

■   ■   ■

Aware of all the stress Mom was under, I determined from an early age not to add to her burdens if I could help it. I developed a sensitivity that made me conscious of other people's needs. I just wanted to be helpful, which is perhaps why I was so impressed by those firefighters who came to Miss Mattie's assistance.

This sense of responsibility for others was heightened when we started going to church at the top of the alley on Williamson Street. Mom began taking us along to Galilee Baptist Church after Dad left and we moved to Rear Snow Street. She found comfort and hope and encouragement there, and so did I. Pretty much whenever the church doors were open, we were there.

I loved going to Sunday school and listening to Sister Jessie Stewart talk about Jesus, then sitting in the worship service to hear Pastor E. Edward Jones Sr. preach. Revival services, when there would be a special emphasis on inviting people to receive Christ as their personal savior, were a regular feature of church life. I was about seven when I felt God speaking directly to me one of those evenings. I knew, even at that young age, that Jesus was real! He was the Son of God who came to Earth, lived a sinless life, died on a cross, and rose again that we might have life. At the end of the service, I walked down the aisle to the front of the church and confessed my faith in Him. The following Sunday, I was baptized.

Being involved at church eased some of the pain of missing my father. After he left Mom, he took up with another woman, in time having two children with her. Over the years my siblings and I have become close with my half-brother, George, who went on to become a pastor in Bossier City, and our half-sister, Clarissa, who is now in Heaven.

Dad would come by Mom's house to visit us from time to time, and we would be so excited to see him. Invariably, he had been drinking, but he never got mean when he was under the influence. A couple of times he brought groceries and made a meal that he ate with us. One of my sweetest memories is when he came around one time with a car he must have borrowed from a friend—because he surely couldn't afford one—and took me and my sister Sheila out for a drive. He picked up a friend and drove to a corner store, where he left the two of us in the car with some snacks while he and his friend hung around on the corner with some other guys, drinking beer and shooting the breeze. We sat there for what seemed like hours before he came back and drove us home, but it felt so special just being in his orbit for a time.

Mostly, though, I was aware of his absence, like there was something lacking in my life. This deep sense of missing out was only exaggerated when he died; I was about seven years old. In addition to his drinking problem, Dad was also a diabetic and didn't take the greatest care of himself. When someone goes into a diabetic coma, the symptoms can seem like they have simply drunk too much. So one night when the police picked him up on the street during a diabetic episode, they dismissed it as his having had a few too many. They left him in a cell to sober up, and he died there, alone, when what he really needed was medical treatment.

Most of the families in our neighborhood did not have a father around, but it was different at Galilee Baptist. Not only were there many families with moms and dads, but more than a few of them were much better off than we were. I developed a practice of getting to church early so I could see these families arrive together. I would stand there in awe as they drove up in their cars. Some were quite fancy (we didn't even own a clunker). The men would get out of the vehicles in their best suits and open the doors for their wives, dressed in their Sunday finest. I would look at them and say to myself, *I sure wish I had a daddy with a car like that and that my mother could wear clothes like that and get her hair done like that.*

Strangely, I didn't feel resentful. Rather, these families were inspirational to me. They gave me a vision of what could be. Meme had a hand in doing the same thing. From time to time, she would take my sisters and me to the grocery store. She had an old man drive her there, and he always took us through white neighborhoods en route, through parts of town we didn't otherwise visit.

I suspect now it was intentional on their part. They wanted us to see that there were parts of Shreveport much nicer than Allendale and that there were homes much bigger and fancier than shotgun houses. My sisters and I were oblivious to that, but we loved to gaze out the window as we drove past these well-kept homes with their well-tended yards. We invented a game called "That's My House." We would take turns claiming a particular property we liked as our own. "That's my house!" we would announce proudly, pointing out the window.

Whenever adults would ask me what I wanted to be when I grew up, I had a clear and definite answer. I would tell them three things: that I wanted to be a firefighter, that I wanted to have a family that was all together, and that I didn't want to be poor no more.

God began preparing me to face the fire ahead through these childhood experiences, igniting my dreams and laying a foundation of faith and patriotism for every age and every stage of my journey.

CHAPTER THREE

Visions in the Sky

Train up a child in the way he should go, and when he
is old, he will not depart from it.

—*Proverbs 22:6 NKJV*

Long before people ever started talking about how it took a village to raise a child, we knew it took a whole neighborhood. Church and community filled some of the holes Mom couldn't plug by herself after she was left to raise six children on her own.

Mom left the dry cleaner and started working in day care. She found a job at Shreveport's Doctors Hospital and worked from 3:00 p.m. to 11:00 p.m., which meant we were left unsupervised when we got home from school. She would fix a meal for us before she left, and we were given strict instructions about homework and chores. Mom expected all the dishes to be done when she got back. Sometimes we would argue about whose turn it was, but if they weren't done, we would all get a whipping.

If things started to get out of hand at home, the phone would ring. Mom would be on the other end of the line, having gotten a call from one of the neighbors, who acted as her ears and eyes. "I know you've got friends round in the house when I have told you not to," she would yell. "Tell them to leave right now." Or, "I know y'all are still outside past when you are supposed to be! You'd better get your butts inside right away, you hear?"

As the peacekeeper in the family, I usually tried to make sure I always did what Mom wanted. But there was one way in which I took advantage of her absence from the house.

We all had to work starting at an early age—not just doing chores around the house, but going out and earning some money as soon as we were old enough. This wasn't so we could have some spending money of our own, but so we could contribute to the family budget; day-care pay didn't go far to support a family of seven.

Linwood Junior High School was a mile or so down the street from where we lived, but there was no school transportation, so Mom would give me thirty cents a day to ride the city bus there and back. She didn't know that I would pocket the money to spend on my favorite snacks—Milk Duds, Snickers, Hershey bars, Chick-O-Sticks—and run the distance instead. Over time I got pretty fast; I usually managed to beat the bus because of its frequent stops. By the time I got to high school, I was a good middle-distance runner—good enough to make the track team, running the mile and the 880-yard dash.

I got my first job outside the house when I was in seventh grade. I'd ride the bus downtown where the *Shreveport Sun* had its offices. This was the scrappy weekly paper that served the city's African American community, and I'd collect a bundle of twenty or so copies. About half of them went to regular subscribers, who would sometimes give me a few extra coins that I got to pocket for myself or offer me a drink or a snack. I was supposed to sell the rest of the copies to whomever I could persuade to buy some, and Mom always insisted I go out and try. It was a stretch for a shy kid, but it forced me out of my shell.

One of my regulars was a friend of Meme's, an elderly woman who spent most of her time sitting in her chair. She would call me inside when I knocked on the screen door, and I would stand there awkwardly while she rocked herself back and forth trying to get enough momentum to rise out of her chair so she could reach her purse. It always made me feel really uncomfortable, standing there while she struggled. I was stringy and scrawny and didn't know how to ask if I might help her up, but something in me wanted one day to be able to assist people like her.

My route took me several miles on foot through some sketchy parts of town. Since I was carrying a stack of papers in my hand, it must have been obvious that I had money on me, but I never had any problems. The only time I ever ran into trouble was one Halloween, when my oldest brother, Raymond, took me out trick-or-treating.

We were on our way home after a very successful evening, carrying all our candy loot in bags tucked inside our jackets. A little more than a block from the house, a bigger, older kid blocked our way on the sidewalk.

"Gimme all your candy," he demanded.

"We don't have any," Raymond protested. I stood quietly and let him do the talking.

The other guy was not impressed. He punched Raymond in the stomach and all the candy fell out from under his jacket, like he was a human piñata. I handed my stash over, too, and we walked home empty-handed and humiliated.

There comes a time when even the most mild-mannered of us can get pushed too far. For me, that time occurred in junior high at Linwood. One of the guys decided my quiet demeanor made me a good target for bullying, so he started pushing me around. I guess it made him feel bigger in front of other people somehow. He'd bump into me and make me drop my books—stuff like that.

Finally, one day it all came to a head—or rather, his nose. We were on the outdoor basketball court when he started in on me again, and I decided enough was enough. Without a doubt, I had a reputation for being meek and lowly, but I knew enough to know that if you were going to take a stand, you had to do so definitively, to let the other party know he or she had stepped over a line.

The fight involved two hits: I hit him hard in the face, and he hit the ground. That was enough. I never had any more trouble out of him, and I learned that I could stand up for myself firmly and fiercely if I had to.

■   ■   ■

Mom drilled Proverbs 22:6 into us kids from an early age. "Train up a child in the way he should go, and when he is old he will not depart from it," she would tell us repeatedly. Even though she quoted the verse to defend her firm hand, it was kind of comforting. Though I did not realize it at the time, it gave me a sense of confidence that my life could go somewhere if I was diligent—that I wasn't simply at the mercy of events beyond my control, adrift in a strong current.

Sometimes I would sit out on the back steps of our house and just gaze up into the sky, thinking that God was up there somewhere. Sometimes, when I stared long enough, I felt like I could see what seemed like two parallel circular tunnels spiraling up to Heaven. Somehow I just knew life was supposed to be better and that somehow, someday, it would be.

Mom did all she could to lay a foundation of faith. Despite the violence and betrayal she experienced in her marriage, she never spoke ill of our father. In addition to ensuring we attended church, she would gather us all together in the living room to sing gospel songs. We were required to take turns praying. I would only see in hindsight how formative all this was and how God was using all the circumstances of my life to prepare me for my future.

Losing my father at a young age was, of course, devastating. I was so small that someone had to lift me up at his funeral to see him in the open casket. I wept inconsolably. Mom did all she could to fill the gap, but there are some things that a woman simply can't give a boy. With my father gone, I had to turn elsewhere to find a role model.

There was his father, Papa Otis. Sometimes the apple doesn't fall far from the tree: he, like my father, had his issues with alcohol and was a bit of a womanizer, marrying three times. And just like my father, he was good-looking with a strong personality. He had a presence about him that drew you in. His rich baritone gave him a commanding presence that I admired—as did his sharp uniform, complete with cap, which he wore with pride as a delivery driver for the Falstaff Brewing Corporation. It may have been manual labor, but it was a job that gave him some stature in the community, and it planted a seed of desire in me to one day wear a uniform that might similarly earn people's respect.

Other male relatives were also quietly influential. Like many black families, mine was both fiercely loyal and also fragmented. It's a commonly mixed trait, woven through the long years of slavery when couples and their children could be separated without recourse and strong black men were made to be breeders but not permitted to be fathers. Our family's roots in Louisiana zig and zag back to a woman named Jane Jefferson, who somehow ended up in the Pelican State after being sold by a slave owner in Virginia—one Thomas Jefferson. Whether she got her last name because she was fathered by the country's third president or merely because he owned her remains unclear.

As they were denied an education, my ancestors' unschooled spelling records their last name in multiple versions that caused them to lose track of one another as they were dispersed through different circumstances. To this day I am still occasionally finding new family connections to Crockroms or Crockerhams or others—though they all share the same pronunciation of "Cochran."

One Cochran with the same spelling as mine left Shreveport for California in the 1940s, taking with him his son, Johnnie Jr. I'm a third cousin to that little boy, who would grow up to become the famous attorney whose representation of victims of police brutality was eclipsed by successfully defending O. J.

Simpson from murder charges in 1995. We would meet for the
first time not long after that sensational verdict, when Johnnie
visited Shreveport for a Cochran family reunion.

Mom's older brother, James, for whom I was given my middle
name, also left Shreveport for California soon after graduating
from high school. He worked as a mailman while his wife, Lil,
was a school teacher. As such, they were moderately
well-off—certainly compared to us—and they seemed to live in
a whole different world, not just a different state. Every couple of
years they would send for Meme to go out there for a vacation,
and she would return with photos of the nice places they took
her. It didn't make me envious so much as proud that we had relatives who had done so well for themselves.

I didn't get to see my Uncle James much—he and Aunt Lil
visited Shreveport rarely—but he made an impact on me from a
distance; he was another successful man in a uniform. Uncle
James and Aunt Lil never had children, and when I became the
first member of our family to go to college, he sent me a check.
In the accompanying letter he told me how proud he was of me.
He wrote that I should always include the initial "J." when I
spelled my name, which I do to this day to acknowledge my
gratitude for both his example and his encouragement.

■   ■   ■

Church and school were two places where I found surrogate
father figures. I was too young then to appreciate how significant
Pastor Jones was in the Civil Rights Movement, or to understand

how Shreveport had figured into the struggle. When I was older, I would learn how Pastor Jones had served as one of Dr. Martin Luther King Jr.'s main liaisons and representatives in Shreveport, where Dr. King spoke in support of a voter-registration drive at Galilee Baptist as a relatively unknown person in August 1958. Five years later, the city made headlines when police broke up a memorial service held for the four girls killed in the infamous bombing at the 16th Street Baptist Church in Birmingham, Alabama.

All I knew as a young boy was that I saw in Pastor Jones and others like him a strength of character combined with gentleness that embodied the best of the Civil Rights Movement. I saw the same in Alphonse Jackson, the principal at Central Elementary School, where we first graders were taught to welcome him with a crisp "Good morning, Mr. Jackson" when he came into the classroom. Though he was short and stocky he carried himself with a dignity that made him seem taller. Well-spoken, he had a quiet authority but also a joyfulness about him that earned him the respect of the community. Another reason I admired him was that he was the father of Lydia Jackson, a classmate on whom I had a quiet crush. Shyness aside, I knew she was in a different social and economic world than me.

Sitting in the pew and at the school desk, my friends and I were taught the best of the Civil Rights Movement's essence—that you couldn't hope to overcome hatred with hatred; all that did was change who the villain was. There was an unyielding resolve about the rightness of equality, but without the ugly desire for revenge. It wasn't about being anti-white; it was about being pro-equality. It was a message of standing for what is right without doing wrong that seeped deeply into my young soul. Along with that, I absorbed an abiding love for my country and what it could and should be, even if it hadn't yet fulfilled all those founding ideals. To me, the gap between the vision of "one nation under God" and the divided reality I experienced wasn't so much something to accept and resent as something to acknowledge and aspire to bridge.

African American History Week was always a big deal. I loved hearing about the heroes and heroines of our past. As someone who enjoyed school, I especially liked hearing about educator Booker T. Washington. I admired George Washington Carver for his name association with our country's first president and, less nobly, for his part in creating a personal favorite: peanut butter.

Then there were sporting giants like Jackie Robinson and Joe Lewis and contemporary figures such as Jesse Jackson. I also was inspired by the example of Ralph Bunche, the son of a barber, who had a distinguished career at Howard University. He played a role in the formation of the Universal Declaration of Human Rights and was awarded the Nobel Peace Prize for his part in helping to resolve Arab-Israeli tensions. To be embarrassingly honest, however, I remember him more because of my situation than for his remarkable contributions. Assigned his example as an African American History Week project in second grade, I was reluctant to stand in front of the class to give my presentation because the pants I had on were so worn that there was a gaping hole in the rear. I was so ashamed. Then my teacher, Miss Hardy, came to the rescue. She adjusted the sash I had to wear bearing Ralph Bunche's name so that it wrapped around me to cover my embarrassment.

■   ■   ■

I was about eight years old when I got shot. I'd gone down to Papa's Fried Chicken on Pierre Avenue, just a couple of streets away, with my friend Tony, who lived a few doors down. I had a rare quarter to buy a portion of Papa's delicious French fries, a real treat. To get there, Tony and I took a shortcut down an alley behind houses on Garden Street.

One of the houses there stood out for two reasons: it was one of only a handful of two-story properties in the area, and it was owned by the only white guy. An older man, he lived there with his wife and never had any contact with any of the neighbors. He and his wife had probably been left behind in the "white flight" that saw others move out of the area. You'd see him occasionally if you walked past, working in the yard or sitting on his porch, but he never spoke.

Tony and I were heading home back up the alley, carrying our food, when a couple of other kids ran past us the other way, from outside the white couple's house. Nothing to cause us any concern, as far as we were aware; maybe they were just playing. Then there was a loud noise. Boom!

I knew it wasn't fireworks, so Tony and I looked at each other and took off, startled. As we raced down the alley toward home, I looked down. There was blood running down both legs. Somehow Tony had not been hit. Because I was panicked, I couldn't feel anything, so I kept sprinting until I reached where the alley met my street, and then I collapsed.

It all happened pretty quickly. Someone carried me home, where Mom grabbed a cloth and started wiping the blood from my legs. By the time she'd wiped one leg, the other would start to leak again from multiple spots. I still wasn't aware of the pain when the ambulance and the police arrived. The EMTs and the officers pushed through the crowd that had assembled, and then I was loaded into the back of the ambulance. As they lifted me inside, I looked over to the other side of the street and saw the old white guy being taken away by police. Apparently, he had unloaded a shotgun at the kids who'd bolted past Tony and me because they had been throwing stuff over the fence into his yard, but he had hit me instead.

Mom was alarmed by everything, naturally, but I was actually excited. I knew I was being taken to Confederate Memorial Hospital, where I had been born. It was only three miles or so away, but it was across a visible neighborhood demarcation—a bridge that separated "the hood" where we lived from the other neighborhood. Although I had seen the bridge in the distance for years, I didn't remember being over on the other side, and now I was going to get to see what was there. When the ambulance reached the hospital and I saw the street sign reading "Kings Highway," the words of a favorite song from Galilee Baptist immediately came to mind:

> *It's a highway to Heaven. None can walk up there but the pure in heart.*
> *It's a highway to Heaven. I am walking up the king's highway.*

Then it hit me. If this was the "Kings Highway," I must have died and gone to Heaven! As it turned out, the buckshot had made a pretty good mess, but it had not done any serious damage. The doctors picked as many of the little BBs out as they could in the emergency department, bandaged me up, and sent me home. There were plenty left behind, however. Fragments would make their way to the surface of my skin from time to time well into adulthood.

I was laid up at home for a few days, during which time I got spoiled with good food and candy treats. Pastor Jones came by to check on me. I got what felt like a hero's reception when I returned to school. I never found out what happened to the guy who had unloaded his shotgun on Tony and me, but there was no big fuss about it in the community as any kind of racial thing. People seemed to figure that justice would be served, and that was enough.

Despite this incident, for the most part I didn't feel unsafe when I was out and about. There was just an unspoken understanding about which parts of town were safe and which were not, when and why it was okay to be there, and when and why it wasn't. Chief among the invisible grids was the line marking the separation between the black and white communities.

Steve and I met to play basketball at what was known as "The Dome," a school sports ground located "'Cross Corbitt," the area that sort of served as the demilitarized zone between the two differently colored worlds. He was the first white kid I'd ever befriended; we'd sat next to each other in class at Caddo Heights Elementary School and discovered a shared love of hoops. One time I crossed the line and went over to his house, where we played outside. His parents weren't unwelcoming, but I somehow just knew never to go back, and Steve never came over to my house. We'd just meet at "The Dome" until he moved away in middle school.

Like so much racism, the rules about what you could do and where you could go were unwritten, but everyone knew them. It just was the way it was. And it seemed to me that the quiet division between black and white became louder as I grew older.

I noticed the subtle shift, a hardening of differences, when I moved on from Caddo Heights Elementary. I'd had my first significant exposure to white people there, making my first serious non-black friend in Steve, and it had been a fairly benign experience. At Linwood Junior High, I found the white students to be less friendly and more reserved, if not outright hostile. Same for some of the teachers.

For the most part, this wasn't out-and-out racism on the part of the kids; that would come later, when they got older. It was more simple prejudice, reflexively echoing what they had been taught until they were old enough to own it for themselves. As such, that meant black and white students could get along and even be friendly enough within limits. Those included not crossing any lines between the sexes. You might think that a white girl was cute, but you would never say so out loud in front of a white guy. Those were fighting words.

The overall cautious acceptance of each other was mostly restricted to the safe space of school. Students who might even have been open to more racial diversity knew it wasn't wise to hang out with someone of another color after school, for their own or their friend's well-being. So when the final bell rang at the end of the day, we each went back to our own worlds.

CHAPTER FOUR

An Invisible Fire

*Consider it pure joy, my brothers and sisters, whenever
you face trials of many kinds, because you know that
the testing of your faith produces perseverance. Let
perseverance finish its work so that you may be mature
and complete, not lacking anything.*

—James 1:2–4

The Promised Land may be flowing with milk and honey, but there's no delivery service for it, no Uber Eats. To get there you have to go through the wilderness. You have to make your own way to lay hold of all that God has in mind, and it's no picnic. Just look at the Hebrew slaves. It took them a long time to possess what God had for them, and not only because of their mistakes. Even when they finally crossed the Jordan after forty years of wandering in the wilderness, they still had to fight for the land God had said was theirs.

Similarly, my boyhood dream of becoming a firefighter didn't just become a reality with no effort on my part. There were obstacles of my own making and barriers put in the way by others that had to be overcome. At times it was a wild ride.

Actually, by the time I graduated from high school in 1978, firefighting was on the back burner. I still thought it would be a great job, but I had gotten redirected, or maybe misdirected, somewhere around ninth grade. It happened when Miss Hudson, the guidance counselor at Woodlawn High School, asked me what I was going to study in college. Her question was encouraging because no one in my family had ever gone on to higher education before. To have her presume I would go was affirming. So I told her I wanted to be an architect.

I knew you didn't need a degree to become a firefighter, so I figured that going on to college to pursue that dream was ruled out. But I'd always had an interest in buildings and design, fueled in part by playing "That's My House" on Meme's shopping trips. And I knew that architecture paid well—I'd made it my second-choice career, behind firefighting, after a career research project in seventh grade. With that ill-considered reasoning and no one at home with any experience or understanding of higher education to help me work things out more clearly, I switched my studies to the courses I would need for a degree in architecture.

Arriving at Louisiana Tech in Ruston at eighteen was a pretty big deal. Although the campus was only sixty miles from Shreveport, it was the farthest I had ever been from home, save for one trip to Six Flags Over Texas in Dallas as a teenager. And I was out from under Mom's roof and supervision.

Things started out well enough the first quarter. I went to all my classes, and I did all my homework, though the challenging math classes I had kept putting off back in high school were tough. Over time, though, my focus began to shift from academics to extracurricular activities. I became a serious partier, more than once ending the night having drunk too much. I'd hug the porcelain in the bathroom and promise God that if He would just get me through the night I would never, ever do that again.

Part of that drift came from just wanting to fit in. When I had the opportunity to pledge for a fraternity, I was all in. At least to begin with. Over time, I began to sour on the frequent shrine meetings with their heavy drinking and hazing—the frat brothers would slap me and my line brothers hard on our bare chests every time we got a test question wrong. The tipping point was the night we were forced to smoke one marijuana joint after another. By this time, I was a serious social drinker, but I had never done drugs. Needless to say, it was more than I could handle. I woke up the following morning in a bathtub, lying in a puddle of my own vomit, my chest bruised purple, and decided that frat life was not for me.

Having limped through the first year, I returned as a sophomore after a summer back in Shreveport intending to apply myself more diligently. Good intentions have to be matched with good habits, however. At the end of that quarter, I received notice that I was on academic probation. Because I didn't really understand the academic world and didn't have anyone in my family who did, I thought that I'd blown my chance at college.

Mom knew something was up when I arrived home with all my stuff and my tail between my legs partway through the school year. I dreaded telling her I had failed. As the first one from our family to go to college, I felt like I had let everyone down. Mom was disappointed but also quite understanding. She welcomed me home, but made it clear I had to go out and get a job.

I was re-employed back in the kitchen at El Chico's, a Mexican restaurant where I'd worked after high school. I knew that wasn't a long-term career move, though, so I also began researching the possibility of joining the military. With Barksdale Air Force Base just over the Texas Street Bridge in Bossier City, on the other side of the Red River, I'd grown up seeing planes coming and going. My three older brothers had all chosen military service after high school, two joining the Army and one going into the Marines, and they had done okay. So I made an appointment to see an Air Force recruiter.

Before that came up, I got a call from the Shreveport Fire Department. Since getting back from Ruston, I had also stirred the embers of my interest in firefighting, and unbeknownst to me, much had happened in the years since I saw those guys tackling the flames at Miss Mattie's.

Like many other fire departments across the country, the Shreveport FD had long been something of an exclusive club. You didn't only have to be white to get hired; for the most part you also needed to be related to or at least know someone who was already part of the department. It was a tight circle, despite the nondiscrimination advances of the Civil Rights Movement. By the time a 1977 federal consent decree forced the city to recruit more blacks, only one of the department's four hundred or so firefighters was African American, expressly hired to avoid the appearance of racism.

So there I was in the kitchen at El Chico's, splattered with hot sauce and chili, when someone passed me the phone. It was Chief Bobby Brooks, and he invited me to interview for a spot in the upcoming Shreveport Fire Department training school class. Half the students in it would be black.

I was beyond excited, and the initial interview went fine. Then I had to sit through a polygraph test, which was just part of the standard procedure. All was going well until the interviewer asked me if I had ever used marijuana. I was worried that if I said yes that would sink my chances, and technically I hadn't done so willingly, or at least not enthusiastically. I tried to make myself stay calm, and I said no.

A week went by, and I heard nothing more. When I called to inquire, I was told that the lie detector had flagged me as deceptive on the weed question. Was there anything I wanted to tell them about that?

I was crushed. I explained what had happened at Louisiana Tech, and how I had been scared that I might get turned down if I had answered truthfully, and how much I wanted to be a firefighter. Then I held my breath.

There was silence for a moment. Then, "Okay, thanks for being straight with us this time. We'll schedule you for the physical agility test."

Grateful and pumped, I turned up at the training academy on Greenwood Road in west Shreveport the following week determined to show the recruiters they had not made a mistake in giving me a chance. I was in fairly good shape and confident I could ace all the timed physical agility tests, like ladder raising and balancing.

The last of the seven exercises was the most demanding: running out, coupling, and dragging three fifty-foot lengths of hose.

I could hear the training officer counting down the time as I pulled, chest heaving. Desperate to beat the clock, I skinned my knees on the asphalt through my pants as I hauled as hard as I could. But my efforts weren't enough.

"Sorry, but you just didn't make it," I was told. "I'm afraid this is going to knock you out of the selection process."

Going home that day was worse than returning from Louisiana Tech. I felt like a complete failure. Seeing how dejected I was, Mom tried to be comforting. Maybe there was something better out there for me, she said.

I spent the next week at El Chico's licking my wounds. Then, out of the blue, I got a call from one of the training officers at the academy. Apparently, whoever had set up my physical agility test had pulled out the wrong hose sizes. They selected three-inch hose, half an inch bigger—and much heavier—than those we were supposed to work with. Did I want to try again? You bet!

■   ■   ■

Having blasted my way through the physical agility test the second time around—I'd trained hard in the preceding days, to make sure I was in my best shape—I was feeling positive when I arrived at the training academy on February 21, 1981. It was great to see that six of my fourteen classmates were black. They included the first woman—of any color—to be accepted. If I and the other black male recruits were to face some obstacles in the days ahead, hers would be doubled.

But my initial confidence faltered pretty quickly. One of the first things our instructors did was take us out to the training ground and the seven-story drill tower. We had to climb the ladder, running up its side as quickly as we could. That's when I discovered I had a fear of heights. A major problem, of course, but up to that point in my life it hadn't been the sort of thing I'd needed to test.

Climbing a ladder is a learned art. You're supposed to take a firm grip but let your arms out a bit, kind of relaxed, then raise the same hand and foot onto the next rung, pull and step up, and repeat on the other side. The higher I got, the more I reflexively clung tight and close to the ladder, almost hugging it. My heart was racing. Somehow, I made it to the top, where you had to climb an overhanging ledge onto the tower roof.

Was I ever embarrassed! One of the training officers spotted my discomfort and took me to one side. He told me not to worry: if I simply followed the technique, I'd get the hang of it. "One thing to remember," he said. "Don't look down! Just look straight ahead." I did what he said next time out, determined to beat the fear. It's amazing what you can do if you put your mind to it, practice, and trust the process. I felt far less nervous on my second ascent, and within a week of repeated climbs—we had to run the ladder daily—I was flying up and over it like Spider-Man.

The academy exposed another area where I needed to overcome some insecurity—shyness. When two firefighters are raising a ladder, it has to be done in unison, kind of like synchronized swimming. The firefighter at the "heel," or what will be the grounded end, has to call out "Ladder up!" for the crew member at the other end to know when to lift, because they can't see behind them. As a quiet kid, raising my voice or drawing attention to myself in any way didn't come naturally. "If you're going to be a firefighter, you are going to have to learn to speak up," one of the training officers told me.

He and the other instructors in the academy—who were all white, save one—made a big impression on me. I respected their knowledge and admired their command of different situations. I thought that, much as I wanted to fight fires myself, one day I might like to have their job. Either way, running into buildings or teaching others how to, I'd have to be more assertive, more prepared to raise my voice. Over time, it became as natural to speak up confidently as it did to run up the side of the training tower. I had no idea how much being prepared to stretch outside my comfort zone like that would prove important in facing the flames many years later.

While I admired my instructors, I also saw in them flashes of bigotry, bias, and the racism I would face at the firehouse. It wasn't overt mostly, but the white instructors interacted differently, more easily, with the white trainees than they did with the black recruits. And then there was an exchange with one of them that revealed more of the ingrained attitude that ran beneath the surface.

Training academy isn't just about learning individual techniques. It is also about learning to work as a team and respect the command structure, which is similar to how the military operates. When you are in a potentially life-threatening situation, someone has to call the shots. Everyone needs to know who is in charge. With that in mind, recruits were supposed to address the training officers as "sir" when speaking to them.

During drill one day, one of the instructors asked me a question and I carelessly answered, "Yeah." I knew as soon as the word came out of my mouth that I was in the wrong. But I wasn't prepared for his response.

"Say that again," he told me.

"Yes, sir," I said.

He gave me a hard look. "That's going to get you in a whole lot of trouble one day, boy."

My blood boiled, but I bit my lip hard. I knew that my lack of respect deserved a slap down, but this was deliberately way out of line. If you grew up in Shreveport—briefly the capital of the Confederacy at the end of the Civil War—you knew without question that "boy" was slave-master language. In addition to being offended, I was also disappointed. This instructor was one of my favorites, and here he was acting with such bigotry. Part of me wanted to challenge it, but I decided this was a test: Was I going to make an issue out of everything?

There is a difference between running away from a fight and choosing not to get drawn into one. I decided to let this racial slur go. There would be a time to take a stand.

■　　■　　■

In some ways, that "boy" exchange prepared me for what was in store when I graduated from the academy five months later, proudly receiving badge 778—one of only a dozen or so blacks out of all the hundreds of firefighters who had served in the Shreveport FD up to that point. As such, I knew that I and my fellow African American graduates had a lot to prove.

There is always a testing period for rookies. It's understandable and even appropriate. Firefighters aren't just sharing an office with a coworker; they are putting themselves at risk in the line of duty. So they need to know they can rely on those alongside them. And that means new arrivals get tested and teased.

Practical jokes were commonplace, like short-sheeting someone's bed. When I was filling in at Station Twelve soon after graduating from the academy, the guys all made a big deal about how much of a fitness nut the captain was and how he expected everyone to exercise regularly and keep in shape. If I wanted to make the captain happy, they said, I needed to run every shift.

Eager to please, I decided to go out straight after completing my fire engine and equipment checklists. The guys told me not to worry if there was a call-out; they'd swing by and pick me up. Sure enough, I was a mile or more from the station when I heard the sirens. I turned round and started heading back to the station as fast as I could. They pulled up beside me, lights flashing, and I jumped onto the tailboard at the back, heading for my first real fire.

The guys thought it was all pretty funny, but I was flustered, feeling foolish standing on the back of the truck in my running gear. One of the guys was holding on to me as I climbed into my bunker gear, which I'd stashed back there just in case. I was already hot and sweaty from having run hard in the afternoon summer sun, so by the time I got all my heavy gear on and we had extinguished the house fire we had been called to extinguish, I was close to heat exhaustion.

I didn't take what had happened too personally. I knew that I needed to earn the guys' trust. However, there is a difference between professional caution and racial hostility, and some people crossed the line.

My reception by C Shift at Station Eight was reserved, but not openly unpleasant. When the other guys made a point of showing me to my bed in the upstairs dorm, I figured it was just because they had their preferred sleeping spaces. Only later, when I got to share experiences with some of the other black rookies, did I realize that a designated "black bed" was the unofficial policy across the department.

The first clear indication of underlying prejudice came after I had been assigned to clean the living room area and the kitchen. I went at it hard, determined to do a good job. I didn't even blanch at having to empty and wash out the spittoons splashed with the spittle from our resident tobacco chewers.

The captain told me there was a problem with one of the other guys, who was on dorm and bathroom duty. He wouldn't clean the bathrooms because after I combed my hair, a few strands were still lying in the sink. The captain told me to go and deal with them so the other firefighter could finish cleaning. What, was the guy scared of getting cooties or something?

I would have been within my rights to refuse. Both the crew member and the captain were wrong—the former for refusing to follow orders, and the latter for failing to insist. But as with the "boy" put-down in the academy, I decided to let it go. Somehow, I felt there would be a more appropriate time to deal with those issues.

This wasn't just a Station Eight thing either. I experienced similar treatment at other firehouses when I filled in as needed on "swing" assignments to cover for guys on leave or out sick, as rookies do for their first couple of years. For instance, out at Station Sixteen, I was given the task of washing the dishes after meals. Like most people, I had done my share of kitchen cleanup at home, but the captain made a point of showing me how he wanted things done there. He ran the water scalding hot, so hot that it was painful to the touch. The silent message was that because of my blackness he wanted to be sure everything I touched was carefully sterilized.

How am I so sure these incidents were racially motivated? Just from the hard-earned experience of growing up in a society that quietly condones prejudice and bigotry, where you learn to read lips that may not move but get pursed. Racism isn't always in your face, but it's always in the air. You can just feel it. It's like the dangerous "invisible fire" threat they warned us about in the training academy; it's one that is quietly burning so hot you can't see a flame with your naked eye. You only become aware of it when you walk into the heat.

It soon became clear to me and the other black firefighters that any disciplinary actions involving us carried tougher penalties than incidents involving whites. It was all part of the "good ol' boys" network that protected its own—like one fire captain who loved duck hunting so much he even went hunting out of season and ended up getting arrested and thrown in jail. Someone in the department marked him down as being "on leave" so that his absence wouldn't count against him and jeopardize his job.

If you had asked most guys outright whether they were racist, I am fairly sure that they would have denied it and that most of them would have meant it. They weren't anti-black, they most likely would have said. They just liked things the way they had always been. They simply didn't recognize—or want to admit—that those old ways were actually racist in nature.

And then there were not infrequent occasions when there was no denying explicitly racist behavior. Some guys would throw the N-word around almost breezily, in reference to specific firefighters or black people in general, without any sense of awkwardness. Some of the guys mockingly called black firefighters "bald eagles," meaning that, like the birds, we were a federally protected species because of the consent decree. All this was simply an accepted part of the department culture; in fact, the second-in-command who used to make station visits freely referred to blacks as "blue gums" or "Jigaboos."

None of this could diminish the satisfaction I got from being a firefighter. And with more fires in some of the black neighborhoods because of poverty—older buildings and people there sometimes having to use candles for light, like we had when I was a kid—it felt good to be serving my community. There is something about knowing you have saved someone's property, maybe even their life, which is uniquely rewarding. And our rescue truck proudly sported a cluster of stork decals on the side—one for each baby we delivered.

Even in the midst of drama there were moments of humor. Once when called out to the scene of a road accident, I found a man in one of the damaged vehicles with a big gash on the side of his head, freshly stitched. "What happened?" I asked him.

"I got shot a few days ago," he told me.

"Well," I said as I checked him over, "I don't know what you are doing with your life, but I sure hope you know Jesus!"

There also were sobering moments where our best efforts were just not enough. I will never forget helping with the overhaul at one house fire, sifting through the debris. We were looking for a twelve-year-old boy who hadn't escaped in time, and I was the one who found his charred body.

This wasn't the first traumatic death I had experienced. That had taken place while I was still at the academy, working a shift in the emergency room at the LSU Hospital Health Sciences Center as part of my EMT training. It was a busy Friday night when we received notice of a gunshot victim en route to the ER. Turned out I knew the person; he was a neighborhood bad guy who lived down the street from Mom, and he was in a bad way.

The lead doctor cracked open the guy's chest and reached in to manually pump his heart, which had stopped beating. After a few squeezes he stopped. "The bullet is in his heart," he said, pronouncing the guy dead. And sure enough, when he pulled the man's heart up out of his chest cavity, there was a thumb-sized bullet hole in it.

Situations like those made the racism I experienced somehow seem even more meaningless. When it came to life-or-death moments, it didn't matter what color anyone was. We didn't know whether someone was black or white or polka-dotted when we responded to a fire or an accident; we just went to help. Nor did it matter what color the other guys on the team were when we arrived at a fire or some other kind of emergency; we had each other's backs all the way.

For me it was almost a biblical calling: After all, Jesus told His disciples, "Greater love has no one than this: to lay down one's life for one's friends" (John 15:13). If we were ready to die together, why did it sometimes seem so hard to live together back at the firehouse? This was why police forces were for the most part much more racially integrated sooner than fire departments; they only had to turn out on duty with each other, not get along with each other in some form of extended everyday life in close overnight quarters.

My reaction to all this was to double down on my efforts to be the best firefighter I could be. I might not have been able to change their opinion of me based on the color of my skin, but I was determined to do everything I could to ensure that when they judged me as a firefighter, they had no choice but to acknowledge I was a good one. Being one of the few guys who was EMT-certified helped, giving me additional opportunities to prove my worth.

I knew I had succeeded after about eighteen months. By that time, I had already earned a coveted spot on the rescue truck. Then one night we were called to a fire at a hole-in-the-wall nightclub in my old neighborhood. No one was in danger, but the place was burning hard.

The captain in charge, an iconic figure in the department who almost everyone looked up to, took me up on the roof with him to hose the flames down from there. "Klein, we've got to get into the attic!" he shouted. Doing this would vent the flames and give us better access. I started hacking at the roof with my ax, and when that wasn't enough, I began kicking with my boots as well. Eventually, I managed to break open a large enough hole to allow us to direct the hose into the attic and tame the blaze. When we got back to the station, the captain told me, "Klein, you've turned into a hell of a firefighter."

I also tried to fit in by serving well around the station. I knew all about keeping things clean from helping out at home, and my time working in a kitchen gave me an edge when it came to preparing meals. I even bought a barbecue smoker, which I couldn't really afford on my starter salary—I had to get a friend to drive me to work until the next payday because I didn't have enough money for gas. I thought I'd finally been accepted when one weekend I was invited to a pool party at one of the guys' homes; I was the only black guy there.

Performance wasn't enough to overcome all prejudice, however. While I loved firefighting, I had never forgotten the impression the training academy instructors had made on me. So when an opportunity opened up to become one of the training officers after three years, I jumped at it.

My student class had been the first to include training for emergency medical technicians, which positioned me well when, just over a year after being promoted to training officer, the center was restructured to expand the city's emergency medical services training. At the time the new organizational setup was proposed, a white training officer was in line for the newly created assistant chief post for EMS training. Because of some delays in the civil service approval process, by the time the position was due to be filled, I had seniority over him, even though I was the youngest and newest training officer. The move would make me the first black chief officer of the department. I waited excitedly for the appointment to be announced, but nothing happened. After several months had gone by with all the other organizational changes implemented, I inquired about the situation.

Oh, I was told, the department had decided that an assistant chief of EMS training was not needed after all—even though all the other areas of higher ranks proposed for restructuring had been implemented. The only difference between me and the others appointed to those positions was that they were white, and I was black.

This time I didn't just let it pass. I gathered the evidence—the sequence of events, the relevant documents, the details of the parallel appointments—and appealed to the Civil Service Board. The board members told me they could see how I might draw the conclusion that I had been discriminated against. But they had spoken with the fire chief, they said, and he had told them that the assistant chief position had been abolished because the budget couldn't support it. Case closed.

Cutting through the disappointment, in my mind I could hear the voices of my childhood "village elders" telling me, "Have faith in God, respect the authority of the Shreveport Fire Department, and treat the other firefighters like you want to be treated."

CHAPTER FIVE

Rekindled!

*Husbands, love your wives, just as Christ loved the
church and gave himself up for her.*

—Ephesians 5:25

There is no denying that some women are drawn to a man in uniform. The experts say it may have something to do with their desire for security and protection; the uniform speaks of discipline and selflessness. That could have had something to do with the way my dating life took off after I became a firefighter, but I suspect there was another factor too. Wearing my SFD uniform, like Papa Otis wore his Falstaff uniform, gave me extra confidence.

I still wasn't a "smooth operator," as the sultry jazz singer Sade would say, but I was aware of and took complete advantage of the way the uniform seemed to make girls want to talk to me. In fact, I'd go to social events on the way home from a shift while still in my uniform to exploit its effect. Sometimes when we were riding on the truck on the way back to the station after a call,

I'd get to shout out to girls passing by if we were in slow traffic and invite them back to the station to continue talking. More than a few accepted the invitation.

Without going into unnecessary detail, let's just say that the first six months of my firefighting career were busy both on and off duty. This was quite a change from the way things had been growing up. Not only was I kind of shy, but I was never good enough at sports to earn the social capital that came with being one of the high school celebrity ballers. Additionally, being poor meant that I couldn't dress as cool as the other guys. Mom tried to help by making me some outfits, and they turned out quite well, but there's no disguising the fact that your clothes don't have designer labels.

Still, I had a few short-lived relationships here and there, but nothing really serious—at least on their part. Being soft-hearted, I was always the one who fell head over heels and was crushed when it came to an end. "Never be the first to say, 'I love you,'" my older brothers warned, but I couldn't stop myself.

So as a rookie firefighter, I felt I was making up for lost time. As part of that, I had moved out of Mom's place. She was increasingly unhappy with my tiptoeing back home very late at night after being out partying. I moved into an apartment with an old friend, Eric, and both of us were enjoying the bachelor life.

Naturally, my spiritual health began to fail. Since I was no longer living at Mom's, it was easier to avoid going to church. Sunday mornings were for recovering from Saturday night, not feeding my soul. I knew the choices I was making weren't good, but they sure were fun, at least in the short term. I kept busy both at work and socially, kind of like the motorist who hears an ominous knocking coming from the engine and turns the radio up to drown out the warning sounds.

It worked for a good while. Being on duty as a rookie took all my attention. Even without calls, there were maintenance, training, and shift duties like cleaning or cooking. In the down-time, when we'd get to relax and watch TV or play games, I'd be on inner alert for the next call, ready to be sure to do my best.

Twenty-four-hour shifts followed by alternate days off left plenty of free time for earning some secondary income; many of the guys had some kind of side job, and I joined the bandwagon for two reasons: the extra money and the extra acceptance from the guys I got to help out. In my off-time I worked construction, roofing, tree clearing—you name it.

With firefighting, moonlighting, and dating, I was a busy guy, but I was young and in the best shape I had ever been in my life. So it was something of a surprise when I woke up in my apartment one morning at the end of a six-day break from the fire station—which had been filled with other activities, mind you—feeling tired. I just knew this all couldn't go on indefinitely.

There was no audible voice from Heaven, no supernatural writing on the bedroom wall, but God spoke to me—an undeniable, clear sense in my heart. *You can't keep doing this,* He said to me. *You've got to get married.*

I may not have been living any sort of a godly life at that stage, but I had enough experience with God in the past to know without a shadow of a doubt that this was Him. And I knew He was right. It was time to stop messing around and put down some foundations in my life if I wanted to build a meaningful future.

When some Christians talk about repentance, they make it seem like a mystical, emotional experience. And there may be some of those elements, but at its core repentance is very concrete, very practical. The word means to do a U-turn, to go 180 degrees in a different direction. You translate what has happened in your heart to what you do with your hands and feet. You act differently. So that's what I did.

Certain that I needed to quit playing around and settle down quickly, I decided that it would take too long to go out and try to find a wife from scratch. That meant any marriage candidate had to already have been in my world at some stage. I decided to make a list of possibilities, tracing back from college days, trusting that when I came across the right one, God would make it clear to me.

I went back over my mental list of all the girls I had known. Those I'd met in the previous six months were immediately disqualified because they were running as fast and loose as I had been. Thinking back further, I mentally revisited the few girls with whom I'd had something of a more serious—or, at least, less carnal—relationship. There was the girl I'd been sweet on during my time at Louisiana Tech. She had been nice, but she'd also had some attitudes from growing up as an only child that made me doubt she'd be a great marriage partner. Then there was my high school crush. I had fallen hard for her, but after we broke up, she went back to the older guy she had dated before. I didn't have a good feeling about that.

Digging back further into my memories, I recalled and rejected the other girls on whom I had been soft. Then I remembered my first-ever girlfriend, way back in elementary school.

Carolyn Marshall came to my mind, and my heart started fluttering like a bird in a cage. She had to be the one.

■　　■　　■

We met in fourth grade at Pierre Avenue Elementary School. She was a newcomer, having just moved into the area from another school district, and most of the other girls ignored her because she was so pretty. So when I struck up the nerve to speak to the cute girl with the ponytails in barrettes on the playground one day, she was grateful to have someone take an interest in her, and things went from there.

It was mostly a playground thing, hanging out together there, but we would hold hands when I walked her home from school. One time her mom came out from their house as we stood on the porch and asked Carolyn who I was. "This is my boyfriend, Kelvin," she said. Her mom looked at me kindly and didn't say anything.

The great romance didn't last long. Her family moved again, and Carolyn transferred to a different school. Our paths crossed again a few years later at Linwood Junior High, by which time she had developed into even more of a beauty. She was further out of my league now—a gap broadened by the fact that not only was my wardrobe plain, but no matter how hard I tried, I couldn't grow out the cool Afros some of the other guys were sporting. Carolyn and I waved as we passed, and that was that.

In high school, she continued on her trajectory of popularity as one of the majorettes. Though we went to different schools, we would bump into each other from time to time at house parties and she would say hello, but that was it.

The last time I had seen Carolyn before my wake-up call had been when I was home from Louisiana Tech for Christmas in my first year. I was out at Mall St. Vincent doing some shopping when I saw her by herself and went over to say hi. We chit-chatted for a while, and then she joked, "Are you here to buy me a gift?"

"Of course I'm here to buy you a gift," I told her. "Where do you want me to get it from?"

"Keepsake Diamonds," she said, naming a jewelry store in the mall.

"Sure," I answered jokingly. "I'll get you a gift from Keepsake Diamonds."

As we parted with a smile, I thought two things: She was more attractive than ever and way out of my league, and I wondered whether she might possibly be a little high-maintenance.

All that did not deter me now. The flutters had convinced me that she was the one, so all I had to do was find her.

Shreveport and Bossier City had small enough populations to have a combined telephone book and Yellow Pages, so I got a hold of a copy and turned to the list of Marshalls. Then I systematically worked my way through them with a simple script:

"Hello there, my name is Kelvin Cochran. I'm trying to find a girlfriend I had in the fourth grade. Her name is Carolyn Marshall. Does she live here?" When they said no, I'd continue, "Well, do you know anybody by that name?"

No and no, down through all the forty or so Marshalls in the book. I was confused more than crestfallen; surely someone might have known her? It didn't occur to me at the time that I maybe sounded just a little bit crazy, calling out of the blue like that. If I had answered a similar inquiry, I probably wouldn't have told the caller anything!

I was down but not out. During my off-time, I took to driving around the Allendale area where we had both grown up. I hoped that maybe one day I'd pass her sitting on a front porch somewhere drinking a cold glass of sugar water, like when we were kids, or at least that I'd see someone who used to know her, and they would be able to point me to her. No such luck.

After about two months of this, I was at a loss. I was still convinced that she was the one, but clueless about what to do. Then I sensed God speaking to me again. *Go check the phone book.*

I pulled it out and turned to the Marshalls page. There was one name without a check mark next to it, and just two initials for the first name—C. F. I must have dismissed it out of hand earlier as being a single guy. This time, I figured I should at least call. A woman answered the phone, and I went through my previous spiel, though with less enthusiasm. I talked about my childhood girlfriend and ended with, "Her name is Carolyn Marshall. Does she live here?"

"This is she."

For a moment, I was stunned. Then I moved into a higher gear, lowering my voice to my best Barry White baritone. I didn't waste any time.

"Carolyn, I'm a firefighter now," I told her. "I have a good job with good benefits. I've been dating like crazy for the last few months. God woke me up one morning and told me I needed to find a wife, and you are the chosen one."

"You must be crazy!"

"No, I'm not crazy. Can I come over and talk to you about it?"

"No, you can't come over here. I have a boyfriend, and he's on the way over here right now."

I was so certain about my mission that I wasn't going to fold and walk away. "Carolyn," I said, "God told me you're going to be my wife. We're going to have a wonderful life. We'll have beautiful children. We'll have a wonderful home. You'll never want for anything."

Maybe it was my determination. Maybe it was because she wanted to see if I was as crazy as I sounded. Whatever it was, she finally told me that her boyfriend would be at work the following night.

"Well, can I come over tomorrow night?"

"Yes."

It was a cold January evening when I knocked at the door of the small Allendale apartment where she was living with her mom. Carolyn welcomed me in, gave me a seat at the table in the kitchen area, and went to make me a mug of hot chocolate.

As she brought it back to set down in front of me, I got out of my chair and went down on one knee.

"Carolyn, will you marry me?"

She placed the mug down, simultaneously shrieking, "Mama, you've got to come in here!"

Carolyn's mother came in, looking uncertain. "Mama," Carolyn told her. "This is Kelvin. I haven't seen him in years. He called me on the phone last night, and I let him come over tonight, and he has just asked me to marry him."

I jumped in, telling Carolyn's mom that I wasn't crazy. I explained how God had spoken to me, and I asked if I could marry her daughter. The fourth-grade flame was rekindled!

■   ■   ■

As the director of a church men's ministry these days, I get to guide young guys through the relationship process. I teach about the four stages we find in the Bible—dating, courtship, engagement, marriage. Each stage is part of the best order of discovery and preparation that sets a couple up for a good life together. Oftentimes it's anywhere from a one-to-two-year journey, and if you or they are not ready to make a commitment at the end of that period, chances are you or the person you're dating never will be.

That process is clearly a long way from the one I followed with Carolyn, so it could be tempting to dismiss my counsel as, "Do as I say, not as I do." However, sharing the rest of our story only underscores the importance of a solid foundation for any couple. Although I believe that for reasons I don't yet fully understand God prompted me to ignore the best way of going about things, it wasn't an entirely smooth happily-ever-after.

Carolyn and I were married at her church, Mount Canaan Baptist, on June 12, 1982, six months after I tracked her down. Talk about a whirlwind romance! It wasn't all roses and moonlight, however. Whirlwinds throw up a lot of stuff. We were learning a lot about each other in a short time—including that her middle name was Fay, hence the C. F. initials in the phone book—and on a couple of occasions, we argued heatedly. At one stage I even wondered whether I should call the whole thing off. But I decided that God was in this, and He would make everything work out. And in due time, He did.

Having quit my bachelor ways cold turkey, I had one wobble, the night before the wedding. It didn't involve girls—just my guy friends and a whole lot of drinking and playing dominoes. So much that we woke up late the next morning. In the rush to get ready and make it to the church on time, I and one of my friends, Malcolm, who was part of the wedding party, got our outfits mixed up. When I got out of the car at the church, I realized I was wearing his pants—which were shorter and tighter than mine. There was no time to change, so I just hoped no one noticed.

For the early years of our marriage, that wedding-day mistake became something of a metaphor. I was showing up, but carelessly, and while most people who didn't look too closely might not have seen anything wrong, I knew there was. And so did Carolyn.

It wasn't all bad, by any means. We had some good times, and we welcomed our first baby, Tiffane, two years after we were married. By the time our son, Kelton, arrived two years later, I had been appointed as a training officer at the academy and was enjoying the new challenges there. We were getting ourselves established. But I was also getting restless. I began to chafe under the commitments at home. I started hanging out with friends after work rather than going straight home.

I moved out when Kelton was about seven months old. I made sure Carolyn was okay financially, but otherwise I looked out only for myself, not even seeing the children much. I was so focused on myself that I couldn't recognize how I was playing out the old family pattern that had so hurt me as a child. Nor did I pause to consider the inconsistency in my character—how at work I'd run into a burning building for someone I didn't even know, while at home I didn't want to be merely inconvenienced by those I claimed were the most important people in the world to me.

After a few months of this, I woke up one morning to an epiphany like the one that had sent me looking for Carolyn in the first place. God spoke to me, clearly and firmly. *You can't keep going down this path. I am not going to allow you to go on living this way without consequences.*

Chastened, I took stock of where and how I had let things slide. I was not proud of myself. I started going to church again, and over time I earned enough trust from Carolyn for her to allow me back home. After the arrival of our third child, Camille, we moved into our first house, a brick ranch style on the west side of Shreveport.

We got involved in church again, and I became more diligent about doing things God's way. Though life was tight financially, I announced that we needed to start tithing, much to Carolyn's initial concern. Almost immediately, we saw evidence of how doing things God's way releases His blessings in our lives.

The state passed a law requiring licensed daycare center staff to complete CPR training. I'd done some voluntary classes for daycare businesses prior to this, and they began to pass my name on to others who needed someone to instruct them. Charging a small fee for the class and a certification card, I soon had a nice little additional income stream. Then I learned that the local General Motors plant was looking for firefighters with EMT training for light weekend safety duties. As one of only a few in the Shreveport FD with EMT skills, I was hired in a heartbeat. Things were looking up.

The reality, however, is that even when we see God's goodness at work in our lives, we can take it for granted. It wasn't until Carolyn and I had been married for more than ten years that I finally fully realized that I was still putting work and my own interests above those of Carolyn and the children. I came to see that I would never find the full satisfaction and joy I was looking for as a man in what I did, but in my relationships with God and my family.

I'd been on the job long enough by then to know that the last kind of emergency a firefighter ever wanted to handle was a rekindle. This is when you've put out the fire—or at least, you think so. But there are some spot fires left somewhere, and sometime after you leave the scene, those glowing embers reignite, so back you go. It means you haven't done your job properly. To avoid a recall, you have to thoroughly investigate the scene, maybe pulling down walls to the studs to ensure there is no hidden danger flickering away in a corner.

In the same way, I needed to check for spot fires in my personal life. I knew the Bible says a man should love his wife as Jesus loves the Church, and I knew I needed to step up and take responsibility for the issues in our marriage. If things were going to change, it had to be me who was going to change. I had to take my life down to the foundations and see what was there.

CHAPTER SIX

The Ladder of Success

Lift not up your horn on high: speak not with a stiff neck. For promotion comes neither from the east, nor from the west, nor from the south. But God is the judge: he puts down one, and sets up another.

—Psalm 75:5–7

I began to strengthen my marriage the same way I earned my credibility as one of Shreveport's first black firefighters—slowly and steadily, knowing that I had to work hard to overcome the reservations I faced. It wasn't what I said that mattered; it was how I performed.

One of the keys to my progress was pressing into my relationship with God. Like many men, deep down I really wanted to do the right thing, but I lacked the ability because I didn't have the structure in my life that I needed. I was like a vine without a trestle to support my growth. Establishing some spiritual disciplines was a game changer, and I began with daily Bible reading.

On our first real family vacation in 1994, we drove to Clinton, Maryland, to visit Carolyn's brother, Joseph, and his wife.

Cruising the highways in our first brand-new vehicle, a 1994 Isuzu Trooper, we made an overnight stop in Atlanta, visiting the King Center to honor Dr. Martin Luther King Jr.'s civil rights legacy. It didn't seem to me that life could get any better, but during our brief time in the city, I did wonder idly what it might be like to be a firefighter in a such a large and vibrant metropolitan area that was so much bigger than Shreveport.

While we were staying with Joseph, I became aware that he would get up early in the morning before everyone else and head down to the basement, where he would sit and read his Bible, underlining passages as he went. I was impressed and intrigued. When I asked him about it, he showed me his One-Year Bible, which included daily New and Old Testament readings, plus passages from the Psalms and Proverbs. "Here," he said, handing it to me, "I want you to have it."

I accepted his gift and committed to reading it daily beginning the following New Year's Day. I started by getting up fifteen minutes earlier than usual to read the allotted passages before going into my day. Over time I set the alarm earlier and earlier as I found myself getting more absorbed by what I was reading.

Having grown up in church, I was already familiar with a lot of the stories, but they began to come alive in a new way. I started to see themes, patterns, and threads that had eluded me before. By the end of that year, I had read through the entire Bible for the first time in my life—and finished my first whole book since leaving high school. Up until that point, all my reading had been on a strictly need-to-know basis—only the relevant pages. Now I couldn't get enough. I found myself studying different biblical words and phrases and their meanings. I began writing down some of my findings and reflections.

My growing awareness and understanding of God were rewards themselves, but there were other benefits. Which is not surprising, of course: the more we live according to His purposes and ways, the more He is able to work in our lives. This isn't about earning His favor and blessings in any way; it's just the simple result of doing things right. When you operate something according to the maker's instructions, it tends to work better!

As I continued to apply myself to putting God first in my life, my marriage and family relationships grew stronger and stronger. And I also saw my firefighting career prosper. I'd already done fairly well, first winning a place on a rescue truck and then a position as a training officer at the academy. But then things stalled, notably when I was deprived of the opportunity of being appointed to the post of assistant chief training officer during an organizational restructuring.

Efforts to correct the injustice failed in my appeal to the Civil Service Board. Subsequently, I just let it go and concentrated on doing as good a job as I could. I trusted God to work things out in His time. A couple of years went by, and then the city appointed a new fire chief: J. Gordon Routley from the Phoenix Fire Department in Arizona, someone from the outside with none of the department's history of favoritism, nepotism, cronyism, and racism. Shortly after his appointment, I met with him and told him about the way things had gone down with the assistant chief training officer designation.

He looked at the evidence I had shared with the Civil Service Board and agreed that I'd been wronged. However, with the passage of time, another white training officer had since joined the academy and now had more seniority than me. If the assistant chief position were to be reinstated, this person would be appointed, not me. I left the meeting feeling vindicated, at least.

Just a couple of weeks later, the training officer with seniority over me abruptly resigned from the department to move out of state with his wife. Once he was officially off the books, I went back to the new chief and reminded him of what he had said. The other man's resignation had once again restored me as the senior training officer; the barrier preventing Chief Routley from correcting the injustice was gone. He was true to his word: he reinstated the position and appointed me Assistant Chief Training Officer of the SFD Training Academy. No sooner had all this taken place than the guy who had resigned changed his mind and returned, hoping to get his job back—along with the new assistant training chief role to which I had been appointed. Too late, he was told. I discovered that when a man is faithful to God and faithful to his family, God will bless his career.

My promotion made history in the department, but it was not celebrated by my colleagues at the academy. They closed their office doors and didn't speak to me for a couple of weeks.

When the city decided to replace two of the training staff take-home vehicles, the chief training officer announced that he would have one of the new ones and the other would go to the other assistant chief of training. Each in turn would pass down their old vehicles to someone down the chain of command. The only problem was that the second vehicle was supposed to come to me because I had seniority.

Either they simply didn't think of me, or they intentionally decided to exclude me. I was surprised when the arrangement was announced in a staff meeting, but I didn't respond publicly. Next day I asked for a private meeting with the chief training officer and the assistant chief who had been named as the recipient of the second vehicle.

Calmly, I told them that I'd been repeatedly ignored for opportunities given to white peers since coming to the academy, and enough was enough. The protocol for new vehicles was clear, and seniority meant that one of the two was mine. The other assistant chief of training hit the roof, standing up and shouting and just managing to swallow a racial slur as he grumbled. The chief of training calmed him down. They had to reluctantly acknowledge that I was right. Getting the keys to the new vehicle was quietly satisfying, more because of the principle than the perk itself. By the grace of God, we grew past those challenges and became great friends.

■　　■　　■

Taking a stand over the new department vehicle was an important line in the sand for me, and the timing was significant. I felt that by now I had earned my place through my performance and that my pushing back on long-held prejudices could not be dismissed or ignored as sour grapes from someone with no credibility.

Confronting the issue was also an example of how my firefighter training bled over into the rest of my life. Through repeated training and countless turnouts to 911 calls, I had learned to calm myself when faced with a crisis. I knew that you could overcome fear—like I did on the academy training tower—by focusing on what was in front of you and not looking down or around. I'd applied that sort of self-discipline to my spiritual development.

I had also learned to lift my voice, as I had been instructed back in the academy. This didn't mean shouting—just speaking clearly and with authority, even if what I had to say didn't make everyone happy. That conviction led me to rock the boat when the department was hit by a hiring freeze. The issue became a political hot potato, and I felt prompted to write a letter to the local newspaper. In it, I warned that if staffing levels didn't increase, it could endanger fire department personnel and also jeopardize public safety because emergency response times would be compromised. Speaking out publicly like that didn't make me popular with the higher-ups in the city administration or some members of the city council, but I later learned that it earned me some credibility within the rank-and-file members of the department, black and white alike.

The thing about convictions is that they have to be held and applied universally. You can't have a sliding scale, because chances are you will let it tilt in your favor. I knew that if I wanted other people to do the right thing, then I had to do the right thing too—no excuses. None of this "one rule for you, one rule for me" business.

One reason that training officers had those department vehicles I mentioned earlier is because we were on call for major fires. We responded to the scenes with a video camera to record the event so we could review and learn from our overall performance, like when a football team assesses plays from its previous game. One night there was a call-out, and for some reason I didn't get the alert. I don't know whether my pager wasn't working or I hadn't switched it on, but I didn't show up at the scene.

When I found out the next morning what had happened, I was furious with myself. I knew that some members of the department looked down a bit on training officers, as though we were not "real" firefighters because we weren't serving at a station. I didn't want to give them any more ammunition to dismiss us. I went to the chief training officer and told him what had happened the previous night and how sorry I was.

He didn't beat me up about it. "Listen, this kind of thing happens, Kelvin," he said. "I get it. Just make sure that it doesn't happen to you again!"

I came away not feeling any better about it all. So I wrote myself a letter of reprimand, took it back to my superior and asked him to sign it. "This is the only way I am going to feel okay about myself," I told him. He looked at me with surprise.

"You're kidding, right?"

"No, Chief—I messed up, and I need to be held accountable."

"Okay," he said with a shrug, signing the letter of reprimand that then went into my personnel file.

I had the same unyielding standard when it came to race. I knew that the prejudice black firefighters still faced was wrong, but cutting them slack as a result didn't make things right. The fire academy requirements were fairly stringent—I knew that personally from having failed the physical admission test the first time around. Once you were accepted for the program, if you failed five of the major exams through the course, you were

out. Cadets weren't just left to sink, however. If they were struggling, the training officers would do what they could to help.
There would be a verbal warning after each failed test. The
fourth time there would be a written warning that the next
failure meant automatic termination. So it wasn't a surprise
when someone was told, "Sorry, we have to let you go."

That job fell to the training officers, and I never enjoyed having to do it. Especially one time, when the black cadet wept and
begged for one more chance. "Please, Chief," he said, "I'll try
harder. I promise." I could see a lot of me in him at his age; he
was heartbroken at having to leave his dream job. Still, I knew
that I had no choice but to let him go and wish him well—even
though I shed a few tears of my own afterward.

It wasn't just about giving the guy another chance. He'd
already had several opportunities to up his game; he had been told
how he was failing and had not been willing or able to make the
grade. To keep him on would have meant we were effectively putting the people of Shreveport at risk by having a less-than-capable
firefighter on duty—and we also would have been denying an
opportunity to someone who might have had a similar desire to
join the department, plus the necessary aptitude and attitude.

On another occasion, as assistant chief training officer, I had
to demote a training officer back to a regular firefighter because
he just did not measure up to performance standards, despite
lots of coaching and opportunities to improve. This one was
especially tough because not only was he black, but he had once
been a member of my church. Still, it was the right thing to do.

As I was learning in my personal life away from the fire
department from growing in my relationship with God, when

you have a standard to follow, right decisions are clear even if they are not necessarily easy or popular. I did not realize it at the time, but this principle was rooting itself deeply in me for future challenges when I would have to decide whether to do the right thing or compromise to avoid difficulty.

■   ■   ■

Just how far I and the Shreveport Fire Department had come in the eighteen years since I graduated from the academy as one of the first black firefighters in its history was evident on August 26, 1999, when I was commissioned as the city's first-ever African American fire chief. I'd ascended through the ranks in far less time than it typically took someone to become a fire chief.

It was a proud moment for me to be introduced to the media at City Hall with Carolyn, our children, my mother, and leaders from all over the black community looking on. Honored as I was, I didn't want to make it about me. In my remarks I ignored the resistance I had faced through the years and praised my colleagues, declaring, "The men and women of our department are so faithful, so committed, that if God dispatched us to Hell, we would put the flames out!"

Even though I was highly qualified for the position, I'd been advised that I would never get the job because Shreveport simply wasn't ready for a black person in that role. That verdict didn't just come from whites, but from prominent black figures as well. In fact, one of the key black political figures in the city told me he was going to put his weight behind appointing a black police chief instead.

That didn't discourage me, nor did it make me want to try to canvass support and make something happen. I was quietly confident that if God had me in mind for fire chief, no one was going to be able to stop that from happening. Over the years I had repeatedly seen how He had been working behind the scenes to bring situations and circumstances together in a way I never could have orchestrated. My part was not to try to direct or control events, but just to ensure that I was walking in step with Him as best as I could in all the areas where He had already given me authority and responsibility—as a son, a husband, a father, a friend, and so on.

Through prayer and Bible study, I had discovered an important principle about the way God works: He does not give divine assignments to men who are unfaithful to Him and their family. When God looks for a man to serve His purposes, the primary qualification is whether that person is being faithful to his family. We see this pattern repeated throughout the Bible: Noah, Abraham, Moses. Each of them proved himself at home before God gave him an assignment. I believe that my career track stalled for a time when I was in the training academy because I was failing in my home life. Only after I began to change there did opportunities start to open up for me again.

That doesn't mean we just get to sit back and wait for God to do everything. We have to remain diligent in what we have been given—and expectant. Ever since becoming a training officer, I had made a point of trying to develop myself. I lobbied to go to the National Fire Academy (NFA) in Emmitsburg, Maryland, making annual trips to keep up with the latest firefighting and training developments and bringing the best of what I learned back to Shreveport.

In 1997, the city agreed to let Wiley College, a historically black university about forty miles away in Marshall, Texas, launch a satellite program at the fire training academy. The opportunity seemed too good to pass up. I enrolled, found some of my Louisiana Tech class credits could transfer, and graduated with a degree in organizational management two years later. That was just before Shreveport began looking for a new fire chief—a position for which I never could have been considered without a degree. Again, God's hand was directing things I could not see.

In addition, when I became fire chief, I realized there were ways I had been preparing for the role without being aware of it. Because of my NFA experience, I had been invited to help lead the department through a long-overdue strategic planning process. In essence, there was no clear sense of priorities for the department—how services should be developed and improved to meet the needs of a growing and changing city.

Along with another fire prevention officer, I was asked to navigate the two-year process, leading a team through reviewing existing operations and recommending strategies for the future. For the first time, we had a document that listed our vision, our mission, our core values, and our organizational priorities.

Knowing that any change would require buy-in across the board if it were to be successful, and because of my experience with being marginalized as a minority, we made a point of giving everyone a voice. We had representatives from each shift and from each division. We included a driver and a firefighter. We had white and black, men and women. We welcomed a union representative. We didn't want anyone to be able to say later that they had been excluded.

This kind of collaborative process isn't easy, but it is transformational. Out of many hours of meetings we came up with what we called the Shreveport Fire Department Organizational Philosophy, the fundamental understanding of who we were and what our role was, agreed upon by everyone. This was not something imposed from the top down, but something all the men and women responsible for making it happen owned.

From that document, we then developed a separate five-year plan to turn the big picture into an operational reality, just before my appointment as fire chief. The timing was perfect. My first task in taking over the leadership of the fire department was to implement the strategic plan—on which the department had already agreed, so it was not like I was coming in and imposing something unknown or unwelcome.

The next eight years were incredibly rewarding. I never ceased to marvel at how God's hand had been on me—from flunking out in my first attempt to join the department, through the years of prejudice and bigotry, to becoming the public face of firefighting for the city of my birth. What a privilege and honor!

There were lots of highs to celebrate—like increasing staff levels and seeing pay rise by one third. Shreveport earned and retained a Class One fire rating from the Insurance Services Office, which is achieved by only a handful of fire departments across the country—which not only recognized our safety record, but also meant reduced premiums for businesses and residents. But most meaningful to me was that during my entire tenure as fire chief we did not suffer a single major firefighter injury or death, and we went almost two years without any fire-related civilian loss of life—something almost unheard-of for a city the size of Shreveport.

Being the first black fire chief brought with it many historical moments. One of them occurred in 2006, the first day of training for a group of newly hired recruits. I had instituted a custom of going to the academy to welcome and challenge them in their quest to become a Shreveport firefighter. There were always relatives of firefighters in every recruit class; as such, I made a point of emphasizing to the new recruits that they were selected on their own merit, not because of who they knew or were related to.

This particular class was different because it included the first young man aspiring to become a second-generation black firefighter, following his father into the department. Seeing Oliver Hollins in the group hoping to become a member of a department that was now one-fourth African American was a reminder of how far we had come from the days where nepotism gave an advantage over other applicants. Oliver would go on to join the department because he earned it, not because his father, Brian Hollins, was the chief training officer.

I'd known Brian since childhood and actually recruited him to join the department while I was in the training academy. Though I was a few years older, we had been friends dating back to our time as kids at Galilee. Brian was like a little brother. He began following in my footsteps when I got him a job at El Chico's. He graduated from the fire academy the same year I did and went on to a noteworthy career, eventually retiring as the academy's chief training officer. His second son, Jordan, also followed him into the fire service.

During my years as Shreveport's fire chief, my profile was rising beyond the city. I had been active in the International Association of Black Professional Firefighters, the Metropolitan Fire Chiefs Association, and the International Association of Fire Chiefs (IAFC). Through this last group, I had met and learned from some of the most-admired fire department leaders in the world. I had been asked to serve in a series of roles that eventually would see me become the first vice president of the organization and take on the presidency—an incredible honor.

The annual IAFC conference in 2009 took me to Atlanta, where I gave a presentation on transforming the culture of a fire department, which drew on my experiences in Shreveport. At the end of the session, several attendees came to tell me they had enjoyed what I had to say. They were from the Atlanta Fire Rescue Department, they told me, and the city was soon going to be looking for a new chief. Might I be interested?

Flattering as it was, I said no; I had too much going on in Shreveport and with my IAFC responsibilities. When the deputy director of human resources at Atlanta's City Hall later contacted me, I agreed to help out by being part of a review panel to interview the final candidates.

While all this was going on, I was following a forty-day "Daniel Fast," eating only fruits and vegetables like the Old Testament character. Over the years I had developed a practice of fasting in one form or another fairly regularly as I sought God's direction in some area of my life. This latest fast had been prompted by a growing sense that, as good as things were in Shreveport, something new was ahead. I just didn't know exactly what.

Shortly after I finished my forty-day observance, I got a call from the human resources officer, updating me on the search for the new Atlanta fire chief. "We've gone through all the candidates and we are down to the final three, but we're still not really satisfied," they said. "We feel like there are better options out there. We were wondering whether you would take a look at the job?"

Things were about to change.

CHAPTER SEVEN

Baptism of Fire

*"For I know the plans I have for you," declares
the LORD, "plans to prosper you and not to
harm you, plans to give you hope and a future."*

—*Jeremiah 29:11 NASB*

There were any number of reasons why it made sense to dismiss the overture from Atlanta. I was due to assume leadership in the IAFC, an opportunity that both excited and humbled me in the way it signaled the respect I had earned among leaders in the global fire service community whom I admired. There was no way I could handle those duties in addition to taking over in Atlanta.

Then there was the question of the wisdom of such a move for my career. Moving to a city and department more than twice the size of Shreveport would considerably heighten the political nature of being fire chief. There had been some of that in Shreveport, of course, but to a much lesser degree than would be the case in Atlanta, with its higher national and cultural profile and media influence as the home of CNN. Plus, the current mayor,

Shirley Franklin, had only two years of her second term remain-
ing, which would mean in all likelihood I'd be looking for a new
job when the administration changed hands, given the political
nature of that kind of post.

And then there was the personal aspect. We knew no one in
Atlanta. Our family was firmly rooted in Shreveport, where we
had recently moved into a new home, and we were active in our
church. Carolyn loved her job as a case management nurse and
liked being close to her mother. We were in a season of harvest
time in our personal and professional lives.

In my humble opinion, I was serving at the pinnacle of my
career, leading the best fire department in the country. I'd
enjoyed a successful tenure—morale was high, and fire deaths
and property losses were down. Shreveport was my dream job!
Looking for another fire chief's job was the furthest thing from
my mind. Prior to becoming chief of the SFD, I'd been
approached about fire chief positions in a couple of other cities.
One I had turned down for family reasons. Another time the
city's mayor had told me plainly, "You're the best candidate for
the job, but we're just not ready for a black fire chief." As I left
his office, I passed three stony-faced senior white officers sitting
in his lobby, looking like they were acting as sentries for the
appointment.

While the challenge of the Atlanta post was appealing, I told
the human resources contact all the reasons I wasn't interested.
She asked me to at least think about it. My greatest surprise came
when I casually mentioned the conversation to Carolyn. She said
I should agree to an interview—not the response I was expecting.

But what if they offered me the job? "Then you should take it," she said, all matter-of-factly.

Taking Carolyn's unexpected openness as a nudge from God, I went to meet the Atlanta city leaders. They asked tough questions, like why did I think my experience in a smaller city had prepared me for a place as challenging as Atlanta? I outlined some of the innovations during my time as fire chief in Shreveport and explained my leadership philosophy: a clear chain of command. I might not be able to learn the name of every one of the Atlanta Fire Rescue Department's 1,100 employees like I had the 400 in Shreveport over the years, but I could be sure that the four deputy chiefs who reported to me knew their jobs, and so on down through the department.

Within about two weeks, I accepted the offer. It still didn't really make any sense naturally—in addition to all the other cons to the move, it would require me to sacrifice a deferred retirement option, essentially giving up a large sum of money that would have accrued to me if I had stayed on in Shreveport and ended my career there. Yet as I prayed about it, I couldn't escape the increasingly clear sense that this was God's leading. I thought of how He told Abram to leave the country he knew and go to a place God would show him and what happened as a result—how that had been part of God's great redemptive plan for the world. I didn't want to miss out on being part of something God had in mind, whatever that might be.

I looked forward to serving Mayor Franklin, whose short stature belied her presence and personality. There has to be a shared respect between a mayor and his or her cabinet members, and I was impressed by her strength and strategic thinking. "Make no mistake, she's always the smartest person in the room," someone had told me during the interview process, and I found that to be true.

I also was really excited about being given the responsibility for helping protect a place with a history entwined by fire and equality—two things so important to me. Much of the city had been burned to the ground at the end of the Civil War, earning it the symbol of the phoenix. As part of that remarkable rising, of course, it became a central part of the Civil Rights Movement, opening the door for me to pursue a firefighting career—even if some people on the other side had tried to keep it closed at times.

Nonetheless, it wasn't easy to leave Shreveport. Over more than a quarter century as a firefighter in the city, I had achieved more than I had ever dreamed as a small boy watching that crew tackle Miss Mattie's house fire. In a farewell letter to the department, I told everyone that the training, education, and experience which had prepared me for the Atlanta position (including the prejudice I had faced, though I didn't name it) had been mine "by the grace of God and the City of Shreveport...I am eternally in the red."

I followed that with a letter to the men and women of the AFRD, introducing myself and laying out my expectations. I knew that I faced a reverse challenge to the one in Shreveport— black firefighters were the majority in Atlanta. I sketched my career advancement and explained my philosophy of making sure everyone in the department had a voice in helping craft its vision, mission, and core values. "Everyone should have an opportunity for input into established rules, regulations, policies, and procedures," I wrote.

"Additionally, for a fire department to be efficient, AFRD leaders shall be responsible for creating a climate where everyone looks forward to coming to work every day; and there are no barriers in the work environment that would hinder them from giving the very best they have to offer," I went on, laying my non-discrimination cards on the table. "Best-in-class fire departments have zero tolerance for harassment, favoritism, racism, nepotism, sexism, or substance abuse in the work place. Boisterous, abusive, and profane language will not be permitted toward any member of Atlanta Fire Rescue."

■　　■　　■

My first cabinet meeting in Atlanta started well enough in January 2008. I was given a minute or so to introduce myself to everyone. I told them how proud I was to serve the great city of Atlanta with them. Then we turned to the agenda, and I discovered that I had signed up for an even greater challenge than I knew. I had a baptism of fire.

If there were economic storm clouds brewing across the country, it turned out that they were already breaking over Atlanta. The city was among the first to begin feeling the effects of the great economic downturn that would follow. As a result, there was a major budget shortfall, and departments were being required to make big cuts. In the fire department's case, that meant slashing twelve million dollars over the coming months. Welcome to the new job!

Needless to say, I was a little taken aback. No one had mentioned any of this in the recruitment process, though the indicators must have been there for them clearly enough. Having experienced several years of continuous growth in Shreveport, I had no reason to suspect things might not be as positive in a larger and more affluent city. I had my work cut out for me.

In effect, it left me with two jobs. My intention had been to focus first on introducing everyone to the philosophy that had shaped the department back in Shreveport—ensuring that there was shared buy-in to our mission, vision, and purpose so we could work on creating the sort of culture I had outlined in my introductory letter. Now I would have to do that while simultaneously tackling the financial crisis—which would mean making tough decisions without having had time to earn a lot of relational trust. It made for some very long days, but I found myself thriving on the challenge. Those first few months in Atlanta were some of the most demanding—but also fulfilling—in my entire career.

I outlined my hopes for the department at a meeting at our airport facility. Since I had first introduced the doctrine in Shreveport, I had been approached by chiefs from other departments who wanted to know how to go through the same process. I had learned how to share it concisely so others could take what we had produced and apply it fairly quickly.

We had thirty-six representatives from across the AFRD at the presentation—crews, civilian personnel, three labor unions, minorities, men, women, and people from the LGBT community. I wanted every interest group to have a seat at the table. It was important that no one could later say they had been excluded. By the time everyone had contributed, we had a list of eighty-four key words for our values on the whiteboard describing who and what the department aspired to be. Over several hours' discussion we narrowed them down. We realized that we couldn't list all the individual concerns that had been raised—favoritism, cronyism, sexism, racism, and so on—without creating an unwieldy document. We agreed on an all-inclusive commitment: we would be "-ism-free."

That became one of the seven core values identified in what became known as the Atlanta Fire Rescue Department Doctrine, created "by and for" its members. Being "-ism-free" was as central and important to who we were as the other six foundational pillars: integrity, competence, excellence, predictability, honesty, and accountability. Indeed, the ten-page document concluded by affirming, "The Atlanta Fire Rescue Department is committed to becoming more diverse, in both personnel and services."

I knew that for all this to really be embraced it had to be more than a paper exercise that was printed, placed in a nice binder, and then tucked away in a drawer somewhere. It had to work its way deep down into the department's daily operations and culture. Over a couple of months, I welcomed personnel from every station to the training academy, where I would spend two to three hours going through the doctrine step by step. To emphasize how serious this was to me, I gave everyone my cell phone number and told them to call me if ever they felt the department was failing to follow the doctrine as it should.

My emphasis on accountability and transparency seemed to be appreciated. One time I was visiting a fire station when the captain pulled me to one side. "Uh, Chief, you know you're violating a policy?"

"Really?"

"Yes, a uniform policy."

He pointed to the bracelet and ring I was wearing on my right hand, in addition to the watch and wedding ring on my left. This had been acceptable dress code back in Shreveport, but in Atlanta the rules were only one ring and a watch. I had slipped up. I thanked the captain for bringing it to my attention, took off the offending ring and bracelet and slipped them into my pocket.

On another occasion I was visiting a station on one of my roving fire chief's office days: once a week I went to a different station and worked from there rather than at the downtown headquarters, as part of an effort to be visible and accountable. If I had any meetings that day, I'd invite the crew to sit in on them if they were free and there were no confidential personnel issues on the table; it was all part of my effort to be transparent. I was a little taken aback when the battalion chief based at the station I was "borrowing" that morning came in to where I was working with a write-up for me. As usual I'd been at my (borrowed) desk by 7:30 a.m., well ahead of my official start time. That was just part of having so much on my plate. However, that was thirty minutes later than the standard 7:00 a.m. start for anyone actually based at the fire station, so the battalion chief decided to call me on it.

This was one time I balked. I explained that, as the fire chief, I had a different schedule, which I was adhering to. "No problem, though," I told him. "In fact, I admire you for what you did. If you're holding the guys here as accountable as you are me, then you're just the kind of leader we want."

Amusing as the encounter was, it also encouraged me that he felt comfortable enough to approach me as he had done. It let me know the doctrine was being embraced. Our leadership culture was spelled out there—predictable, visible, accessible, approachable, and accountable—and the battalion chief had felt empowered to test it.

What many people maybe didn't realize was how much of what I had presented and what had been accepted in the doctrine was based on biblical truth. I didn't footnote everything with a Scripture verse, but the principles and practices were drawn from my years of studying the Bible—excellence, honor, sacrifice, and so on.

It wasn't that I was trying to sneak God into the department without anyone realizing it. I'd never hidden my faith back in Shreveport, and I didn't when I arrived in Atlanta. I did realize, however, that even with its many large congregations and rich church history, Atlanta overall was more diverse culturally and religiously than Shreveport, so I tried to be sensitive to that by focusing on what we shared in common rather than what we might differ over. In Shreveport, meals at the firehouse had always been preceded by grace, and as I advanced I would routinely begin meetings with a prayer, even as fire chief. I stopped doing that as a matter of course in Atlanta, but I would still do so occasionally when it seemed appropriate. No one objected, either directly or via the confidential integrity line the city maintained in order to allow employees to air grievances without fear of retribution.

As we grappled with the budget cuts, I even invited members of the department to join me in a fast. Speaking at an executive

staff meeting at the start of the new financial year, I said I knew
that we came from different faith backgrounds, or none, but that
when Christians seek particular wisdom and help, we will sometimes fast. "We've come through a lot and we have a tough year
ahead, so I'm committing to a fast and I'm calling members of
the department to join me in whatever way they may like," I said.
Several people told me they'd be joining me.

■   ■   ■

To add to all the pressure of those first few months in Atlanta,
the city's financial headache worsened. I was told that the cuts
in the fire department needed to go deeper than initially
thought—to a total of fifteen million dollars. There was no way
to trim that sort of spending without making people unhappy,
both members of the department and the public alike. The challenge was to make the hard calls as graciously as possible.

Working from calls, response times, and other service data,
we came up with a list of stations for blackout and brownout.
Blackout was permanent closure. Brownout meant mothballing
operations for a time, with the aim of bringing the station back
into service when finances permitted.

One of the toughest decisions was to close Station Seven, the
oldest in the city. Opened in the West End in 1894 and known
as "The Rock," it was a fairly busy firehouse, but its call volume
couldn't be considered in isolation. Over the years, other stations
had opened in surrounding communities. Because of their loca-
tion, they could more easily cover for the loss of Station Seven
than if one of them were to be shuttered. Response times would

still increase a little, but not as much as if one of the other stations were to go.

Still, it wasn't a popular decision. Opposition to the plan was fueled by the fact that Station Seven was in a predominantly black community while another station in the north of the city that was earmarked for only brownout had a lower call volume—and was located in an affluent white area. The rationale had nothing to do with race, but some people didn't see things that way.

Having a black fire chief come to the area and explain the process helped, but it still wasn't easy. I went to West End public meetings where I acknowledged how residents must be feeling. I spoke about how the station had served four generations of Atlantans—including the grandparents and great-grandparents of those I was addressing. "These firefighters have resuscitated your husbands, delivered your babies, put out your fires," I said. "I know there's no amount of science and data I can show you that's going to make you feel any better about closing this station."

Nonetheless, I tried to explain some of the reasoning. I talked about how times had changed. When those first fire stations had been built, they were situated about a mile and a half apart, based on the response time of horse-drawn wagons. Motorized vehicles could get to calls quicker now, of course, even with the heavier city traffic, so stations didn't need to be as close. People still weren't pleased, but they accepted that the decision was based on sound justification.

I felt that it was important to recognize the community's great sense of loss. Rather than just shut the doors of Station

Seven and leave, I suggested we have a formal decommissioning service and invite members of the public. Mayor Franklin attended. We celebrated the station's history and recognized the important contribution it had made to the community.

Not every decision I made was about taking things away. Something I added was an annual conference for the department's fifty or so female firefighters. It was another way of communicating that I was serious about no -isms, including sexism. It provided a space for them to raise issues of concern to them as minorities in a heavily male environment. I wanted them to know that I wasn't just paying lip service to fair treatment for everyone.

The budget-cutting process made me aware of the heightened political stakes in Atlanta. Even small towns have their personalities and political currents that have to be navigated, and I had experienced my share of them in Shreveport. But I found myself dealing with a whole other level of that in Atlanta—not only with the public, but also with the city government and within the department itself.

Leading everyone through the AFRD Doctrine process had been helpful in broadly uniting us all around a shared vision and values. But you can't eliminate all conflict. One of my four deputy fire chiefs had applied for the fire chief position before I was selected, and I knew she was disappointed not to get it. I had no complaints about the way she did her job, but I sensed a bit of resentment toward me.

Aware of the resistance to the appointment of an outsider like me to serve as fire chief, I had determined to develop leaders in such a way that, in the future, candidates from within the AFRD would have a better shot at the top job. This would require some changes, including bringing an end to a long-standing culture of internal division and strife. Additionally, there needed to be a more rigorous approach to professional development that would make senior officers better candidates. As part of that, I mandated that all chiefs attend at least one class at the National Fire Academy every year. I knew from personal experience that this would not only be beneficial to the department, but also would help sharpen their résumés. I also instituted job rotation among the four deputy chiefs so they would gain experience in each of the department's four areas: field operations, airport operations, support services, and technical services.

The deputy chief candidate over whom I had been selected had a strong personal relationship with one of the most influential members of the city council. When I was called to a meeting with that council member one day, I was surprised to find the deputy chief in the office too. The council member said she wanted me to do her a favor: She wanted me to start giving her deputy chief friend a higher profile at city council and public safety meetings.

That was a bitter pill I could not swallow. Playing favorites meant I would be choosing one person over another for reasons that violated my core value of being "-ism-free." Personal preference without any objective standard is prejudice, and my commitment to principled leadership allowed no room for cronyism. I told the council member that the deputy chief was free to attend any meetings when her schedule permitted, and I would of course want her to present anything that related to her area of responsibility, but beyond that I could not, and would not, create any artificial opportunities for a higher public profile.

In principled leadership, there are things we stand for and things we just won't. I knew my response to this request was not going to win me any favor with the council member, which would make my position even more insecure when the current administration came to an end. Nor would it endear me further to my deputy chief. But I just wasn't going to play that kind of politics. I trusted that if I did what I knew to be the right thing, then God would work things out when the time came.

That busy year-plus was the most challenging season of my career, but I pressed into my relationship with God like never before. His hand was heavy upon me and strengthened me through it all—but it wasn't quite over yet.

CHAPTER EIGHT

America's Fire Chief

The LORD will make you the head, not the tail. If you pay attention to the commands of the LORD your God that I give you this day and carefully follow them, you will always be at the top, never at the bottom.

—*Deuteronomy 28:13*

Even when you are confident that you are in the center of God's will for your life, things don't always go smoothly. The first few months in Atlanta were a whirlwind of activity, and although I thrived on the work challenge, the long days created some strains on the home front.

Carolyn's encouragement had been a critical part of my pursuing the fire chief job in the first place, but now that I had it, she was finding the transition extremely difficult. In addition to being away from family, she was intimidated by the heavy Atlanta traffic and was reluctant to venture out on her own. That meant she spent long hours alone until I returned home in the evening—often pretty wiped out. I'd offer to take her out to explore the area, which we also did on the weekends. I seemed to be on the go nonstop.

One Saturday I felt like I really needed a down day when I could just kick back, watch some old TV favorites, and recharge my batteries. I got up early to knock out the few honey-dos that were on my list while Carolyn was still sleeping, then settled down in my sweats with the remote control in hand.

When Carolyn came down and asked me to take her someplace, I sighed. "Honey," I said, "can I just have one day to myself?"

She disappeared, and I turned back to my shows. An hour or so later, I realized that Carolyn had not come downstairs again. I went up to look for her. She was standing by the window, tears streaming down her face.

"Hey, what's wrong?" I asked.

"I think we made a mistake in coming here," she said.

I felt terrible. I realized that I had been so caught up in all the demands that were being made of me and all that I was doing that I had lost sight of the price Carolyn had paid in the move. I was failing to put my family first. I had to admit that I hadn't been loving my wife in the way the Bible calls us to—sacrificially. From that day on I determined to put her needs ahead of my own.

Over time, Carolyn began to feel more at home. She started to venture out in the car. One day I came home from work and found the house empty. I called her cell phone to ask where she was. "At Lenox Mall," she told me triumphantly. Not long after, one morning as I was leaving for the office, she said, "I'm going to find a job today." That same evening when I came home, she announced her new job as a case management nurse at Emory University Hospital.

Finding ourselves a church home was an important development too, though that wasn't all smooth sailing. Having watched television broadcasts of some of the amazing churches in the Atlanta area while in Shreveport, I'd imagined it would not be hard to find a place where we felt comfortable. But although we felt welcomed, we just didn't sense a real connection at any of the churches we visited. After several weeks of this uncertainty, Carolyn told me she was going to trust my judgment on where we should settle. She was confident God would speak to me.

Given her typical desire to be involved in making decisions, I took this to mean she was handing me the baton—so I ran with it. One Sunday we visited Elizabeth Baptist Church, which was only a couple of miles from our home. We had been there before, when we had driven all over the greater Atlanta area to visit possible churches. This particular morning, Dr. Craig L. Oliver Sr., only the church's sixth pastor in its eighty-year history, spoke about trusting God over our natural senses and judgment. He called it "canceling carnal calculations"—a phrase that stuck with me.

When he invited anyone who wanted to make Elizabeth Baptist their church home to come forward, I knew God was telling us this was where we were supposed to put down our roots. It felt like a divine moment when I got up and walked down to the front of the church to signal my decision—until I looked back and saw Carolyn's face. She was clearly not happy.

Out in the car after the service, an angry Carolyn told me I shouldn't have done that without telling her first. I was a little bewildered—I reminded her that she'd told me a couple of weeks previously that she was leaving me to decide where God was leading us. Having said that, I wasn't going to insist she make a decision of her own if she was not yet ready; I didn't want her to feel obligated, I tried to explain. But when I felt God speaking to me, I had no choice but to respond; that's why I had gone forward alone, to give her time and space.

Having worked through that misunderstanding, Carolyn walked forward at the following week's service, and we began to make a home at Elizabeth Baptist Church. Everyone was very warm, and we quickly began to feel like family. Going through the new members class together was special and accelerated our growth together as a couple. It was the first time in our twenty-five years of marriage that we'd really gotten to study and learn alongside each other; back in Shreveport, we had attended services together, of course, but had never been in the same Sunday school class because I was often teaching one.

There was one other personal highlight in that professionally stretching first year in Atlanta. Carolyn and I leaped for joy on November 4, 2008, as we watched the election night returns on television: Barack Obama would be America's first black president. I had always believed the country would elect a black president one day. I just was not sure, given the prejudice I had experienced through my firefighting career, that it would happen in my lifetime.

The next morning, I left the house early to drive by the King Center on my way to the office. No one else was there when I parked and walked over to Dr. King's tomb, the eternal flame flickering nearby. Standing there in my uniform, I wept tears of joy and sadness as I thought of all I owed to him and so many others who had given their lives—many literally—so that I and others like me could fully enjoy the freedoms our country espoused.

I thought back to how I'd visited here years before on our first family vacation, as an assistant fire chief, wondering what it might be like to serve in such a wonderful city. And here I was now as its fire chief, one of the "dream children"—the first generation of beneficiaries of Dr. King's famous "I Have a Dream" speech, where we are judged by the content of our character rather than the color of our skin. Through many dangers, toils, and snares, I realized I was now in "The Promised Land" he had foreseen.

I couldn't imagine ever feeling more proud—until I found myself not only celebrating the election of America's first black president, but being invited to serve in his administration.

■   ■   ■

I was driving to visit a fire station one sunny March day in 2009 when I received a call from a White House staffer. He indicated that President Obama was assembling his administration and asked if I was interested in serving him as the United States fire administrator.

This was an almost unbelievable invitation—not only to be part of making history in President Obama's first term, but to hold what was recognized as the highest fire service office in the nation, effectively "America's Fire Chief." Seriously—they wanted the poor kid from Shreveport who only ever wanted to be like those heroes he saw fighting Miss Mattie's fire? I learned later that my track record of service had been one of the reasons I had been suggested for the position. In a news article about my appointment, an Atlanta council member noted that I had been "cool under pressure" during my challenging time in the city.

The White House caller seemed a little surprised when I didn't shout "Yes!" down the line. Humbled as I was by the inquiry, I explained my hesitation. I'd only been in Atlanta fourteen months or so during a very challenging time for the department. Despite all we had achieved, there was still plenty to be done. I'd feel a little like I was abandoning everyone if I left now. Then there was domestic life: Carolyn and I were finally settled and happy. I didn't want to ask her to sacrifice so much again.

The caller said I had three days to decide; he would be back in touch on Sunday. Surprising me once again with her generosity and openness, Carolyn told me how proud she was of me and that I should definitely consider the invitation.

I'd never been one to walk away from a challenge, and I didn't want to start doing so now. Mayor Franklin's second term was coming to a close at the end of the year, and I had accepted the Atlanta position knowing I might be on my way out when she left. But I decided that if there was any way I might stay on as fire chief under the new administration, then I needed to remain in Atlanta to see the department through some of the changes and innovations I had initiated.

Having prayed about it, I felt led to contact the three main front runners in the city's mayoral race. If they each said they planned to keep me on, I would take that as a sign from God to stay where I was and tell President Obama's representative, "Thank you, but no thanks."

First on the list was the council member with whom I had clashed over her request for me to give preferential treatment to one of my deputy chiefs. I told her what was happening, confidentially, and how I felt I should stay in Atlanta if that was an option. She congratulated me, then asked how could I even consider turning down such an opportunity? And to be honest, she hadn't thought as far ahead as cabinet appointments should she become mayor, she said.

Next was another council member with whom I'd had a good working relationship. She also told me congratulations but said it was too early for her to be thinking about specifics like the fire chief.

That left the third candidate, Kasim Reed, who had been a Georgia state legislator for the past seven years. I'd had no direct contact with him, but I knew he was a rising political star. I played phone tag with his office staff for the next couple of days, but I never did get to speak to him before the White House called back. That settled things for me.

"I would be honored to accept that invitation," I told the caller that Sunday afternoon. Taking a pay cut and losing a departmental vehicle seemed like a small sacrifice to make for such an opportunity.

There is no such thing as a slam dunk in government, however. Having met with Janet Napolitano, the secretary of the Department of Homeland Security, under which the fire service position fell, and having been approved for the position, I then had to pass the detailed vetting process. I worried a little about what some of my old college friends might say about what I was like back then, but they must have spoken well of me, or else the investigators dismissed that period as my being young and dumb.

While I waited for the results of the inquiry, I thought back on all that had happened in my life and how God's hand had been on me, nudging and directing me even at times when I was not aware of it—among them, when I first became fire chief back in Shreveport.

The promotion had come with a salary I had never experienced before, and I knew I was out of my league when it came to handling my taxes. Someone recommended an accountant who could help me. He made several proposals that could reduce my obligations, one of which just didn't sit right with me for some reason. I was no tax expert, but it just felt like I would be pushing my luck with the move he suggested. I told him I didn't want to do that, thanks. "I could be competing for a federal government position one day, and I don't want this to come back on me," I had said. I didn't know where that thought had come from at the time, but now it seemed to be another example of God's unrecognized guidance.

Having been drilled hard for my Senate hearing appearance before the Committee on Homeland Security and Governmental Affairs, I was relieved by the way it went. Senator Joe Lieberman, the committee chairman, welcomed me by noting that my record was "a classic Horatio Alger or American Dream success story, and they are always inspiring for us to see come before the Committee."

There were a couple of light moments in the hearing. Senator Tom Coburn wanted to know if the two young women sitting behind me were my daughters. I explained that I did have two daughters but only one of them, Tiffane, was with me. The other person was my wife, Carolyn.

He also asked me about my desire to serve others. "Well, the major part of that comes from my faith," I answered. "I just believe that is why I was born—to serve—and one of the strange consequences of a relentless desire to serve is being promoted to higher levels to be able to serve at a greater capacity and to be able to serve more people. I think that the more lowly you are in servanthood, the greater the opportunities that will come your way."

Before the hearing concluded—with my unanimous confirmation announced two days later—I had an unexpected opportunity to demonstrate some of the firefighting experience I had spoken about. As Senator Susan Collins asked me what the U.S. Fire Administration might do under my leadership to help decrease the loss of life and property, bells started to ring outside the hearing room.

"That is a great question, Senator," I said, "but I have to ask: Was that a fire alarm that we just heard?" There was laughter as she explained the bells were announcing a quorum call, not an emergency.

"I can relax," I said.

"But we would look to you if, in fact, we had to evacuate," Senator Collins said.

"I am prepared to lead us if that is the case," I told her, before we went back to the hearing questions.

■   ■   ■

If my appointment as fire chief of Atlanta had been like a child-hood dream come to life, then becoming U.S. fire administrator—the first black firefighter to hold the position—also took me back to being a boy. When I was young, I had been so excited the night before a school field trip that I could barely sleep. And that's what it was like every day on the commute to my office on C Street in downtown Washington, D.C., at the Federal Emergency Management Agency (FEMA) headquarters.

Founded in 1974, the U.S. Fire Administration was birthed out of the landmark "America Burning" report that shocked everyone by estimating there were twelve thousand fire deaths and three hundred thousand serious injuries each year in the United States, along with property losses of more than eleven billion dollars. Recognizing that thousands of independent fire departments across the country had little or no coordination or communication between them, the report called for some sort of national effort to reduce losses of life and property due to fire.

Central to that attempt was the development of standardized training across all levels, much of it at the National Fire Academy, where I had learned so much during my career. In addition, the administration was responsible for overseeing fire safety and prevention measures aimed at helping the public reduce danger and damage. Also charged with coordinating large-scale responses to situations beyond the capacity of a single city or even state to handle—whether that's a natural disaster or a terrorist attack—the administration became part of FEMA, which in turn was folded into the Department of Homeland Security following 9/11.

Going to work in the heart of the nation's capital was always a thrill, but I found it just as rewarding to head out to the National Fire Academy in Emmitsburg, about an hour's drive from where we lived. I made a point of working from there at least once a week, similar to the way I had gone to different fire stations in Atlanta. I knew how foundational my time at the academy had been, and I wanted my presence there to help affirm the importance of the center. In addition to my regular meetings and commitments, I would audit classes and try to be there when the latest group was graduating.

One of my first tasks was to integrate fire service doctrine into the culture of the USFA, crystallizing and clarifying our purpose and vision. From there we could continue developing the strategic plan for the administration that my predecessor had begun but not completed. This was organizational planning at a whole other level—not just for a fire department, but for coordinating with other national agencies such as the U.S. Forest Service, which has its own firefighting service. I also inherited the task of furthering the fire service's role in the new National Response Framework, a nationwide incident-management system developed in the wake of the 9/11 attacks and Hurricane Katrina's devastation of New Orleans—two catastrophes that had revealed big gaps in our response capabilities for major events.

Firefighting has come a long way since the first volunteer fire company was formed in Philadelphia back in 1736. Equipment and techniques have advanced, as have the challenges brought by dense cities, industrial complexes, and the threat of terrorism. The 9/11 attacks in New York City and Washington, D.C., highlighted to the world what those of us in the profession had always known—how dangerous it was. But until then, no one ever could have imagined that 343 firefighters would be lost in one day, or a time when 15,000 firefighters mobilized from within the City of New York to respond to an incident would not be enough.

Though I had been far from the World Trade Center on September 11, 2001, I was drawn into the swirl of events on that terrible day. Serving as fire chief in Shreveport at the time, I was on my way to Station Sixteen for a visit when a message came through my pager that a plane had hit one of the towers. When I arrived, the crew was gathered around a television, where we saw the second plane crash into the other tower.

Knowing this was a major incident, I contacted the dispatch center and activated the city's emergency operations center, summoning all department heads. As we gathered, we learned there was heightened need for our being on full alert: Air Force One had brought President George W. Bush to Barksdale Air Force Base, which was just across the river, after he had been informed of the attacks while visiting a school in Sarasota, Florida.

Some weeks later, we organized a public safety memorial service to honor those who had died in the attacks. I arranged for 343 members of the Shreveport and area fire departments to dress in their bunker gear and sit together in a designated section of the auditorium. It was a sobering visual reminder of just how many firefighters had been lost that day.

In my brief remarks, I took an opportunity to recognize the sacrifice so many had made and also to make an appeal. I noted how remembrances like the one we were holding touched people deeply. "They can give the impression that the greatest honor in our proud profession is dying together as brothers and sisters in the line of duty," I said. "The greatest honor for our profession is not dying together as brothers and sisters in the line of duty, but living together as brothers and sisters in the line of duty."

While I was referring to an end to prejudice, I also had in mind avoidable loss of life. I remembered the first firefighter I knew to die in the line of duty. Percy Johnson, the second black training officer in Shreveport, had succumbed to burns sustained in an explosion at the Dixie Cold Storage Company. He and another training officer, who was permanently disabled in the blast, went in to try to tackle a dangerous anhydrous ammonia leak because they were part of the department's specialized hazmat team. Percy's death had left the training officer vacancy I had filled.

Both men had been as careful as they could be, but I knew of times firefighters had taken unnecessary risks, and as fire chief in Shreveport and Atlanta and now as the U.S. fire administrator, I would do all I could to enhance firefighter safety. No one becomes a firefighter looking to die, but there is an element of the job—that heroic image that had first captured my attention as a small boy—that can cloud your judgment if you are not careful. When the flames are dancing, the bells are ringing, and the adrenaline is pumping, trained caution can give way to unnecessary risk-taking. I got that. When I was a rookie, we typically didn't wear our breathing apparatus because it wasn't considered "courageous" until it was made a disciplinary issue.

But when I was put in a position of leadership, I didn't want to be the one to have to inform family members that their firefighter had been injured or, even worse, lost as result of reckless behavior. It's one thing to pay the ultimate price when you have run a serious cost-benefit analysis and decided that it's worth putting everything on the line. It's another to be foolish. You don't send someone into a compromised burning building if you know there's no one inside. All that meant insisting everyone followed the rules, even if some in the department murmured that I was more of a paper-pusher than a real firefighter. I would tell crews repeatedly that I wanted everyone to get to go home at the end of a shift. "There's a thin line between a medal of valor and a thirty-day suspension," I would say.

I was keenly reminded of the high price firefighters could pay every time I was at the National Fire Academy. Whenever a fighter died in the line of duty somewhere in the country, the flags around the National Fallen Firefighters Memorial at the academy would be lowered to half-mast for thirty days. The days they flew higher were fewer than those they were lowered.

As U.S. fire administrator, I was keen to use whatever influence I had to help reduce line-of-duty deaths and injuries. Not only did that mean tackling the remnants of the risk-taking, daredevil culture, but it also meant promoting professional development— something I had always believed in. Because of resistance from most labor unions, once a firefighter graduated from the recruit academy, they did not need to take any physical fitness tests again, unlike the military. Invariably, some firefighters would get out of shape over time and find themselves unable to meet the physical demands of the job—as the high incidence of fatal heart attacks attested year after year. I hoped to change that during my time in the nation's capital.

Serving at the highest level of my calling, I began to see how God in His sovereignty had used every job and promotion, from the *Shreveport Sun* to fire chief of Atlanta, to prepare me for the U.S. Fire Administration. But He still had more in store in the months ahead.

CHAPTER NINE

A Safer City

Unless the LORD builds the house, the builders
labor in vain. Unless the LORD watches
over the city, the guards stand watch in vain.

—Psalm 127:1

I was having the time of my life as U.S. fire administrator when I got a call from the deputy director of human resources in Atlanta in January 2010. Kasim Reed had won the mayoral election and was building his cabinet. The HR rep wanted to pick my brains about finding the city a new fire chief. There had been no permanent replacement after I left because of the impending change of administration.

I talked him through the main criteria I felt were important in choosing the right person: a heart for servant leadership; embracing diversity, authenticity, and reliability; and an ability to articulate and communicate a clear vision.

"Sounds to me like we need another Kelvin Cochran," he said with a chuckle. Then he asked, "Would you be interested in coming back at all?"

"I don't know," I said. "Possibly."

The HR person sounded surprised. "Seriously?"

"Well, nothing's ever entirely off the table," I said.

I was serious, but I wasn't necessarily looking to leave my desk in the capital. I was at the pinnacle of personal and professional achievement, and moreover, I had been in the role only a matter of months.

All of which may make my response to the HR officer sound surprising, but it came from my experience of God's leading and guiding in the past. I knew that sometimes He works in ways that do not always make sense to us; we just have to be sure to follow what He tells us and trust Him for the rest.

My openness to that question led to a follow-up call from Atlanta's deputy chief operating officer. Mayor Reed was going to be in Washington, D.C., soon for an appointment with President Obama, and he wanted to meet with me.

I caught a cab to the downtown Hilton, where Mayor Reed's staff had arranged for a private meeting room. We talked for thirty minutes or so, during which time I had my first encounter with Atlanta's dynamic new leader. I could see why he'd been voted into office.

Mayor Reed was charismatic—sharply but not flashily dressed. He carried himself with a sense of quiet authority and confidence, speaking clearly and warmly, recalling how we'd tried to reach each other a few months earlier but had failed to connect. Like a good politician, he warmed me up before he made his pitch.

He told me that as a state senator, he had followed goings-on in Atlanta and had been impressed with the way I had handled the big budget cuts the fire department had to deal with—not just the decisions that had to be made, but also how I had communicated with the media and the general public.

Mayor Reed shared his vision and goals for his time in office, how he intended to make public safety his highest priority. He wanted Atlanta to be the safest city in America. Having the reputation of "a safer city" would attract more business to Atlanta and cause it to prosper, he said. As part of all that, he was going to restore all the cuts that had been made to the fire department, he said—including reopening Fire Station Seven. "I need the best fire chief and the best police chief in the country," he told me, "and you're the best fire chief. Name your price."

I wasn't sold on taking the job, but I gave him a figure that took into account the pay cut I'd taken upon leaving Atlanta for Washington, D.C. He didn't blink. "Consider it done," he said.

I told him I'd think about it all further, and that I needed to speak with my wife about it—considering how critical Carolyn's input had been previously in discerning God's direction.

Upon arriving home, I couldn't wait to share the encounter with Carolyn. She jumped for joy. "When do we start packing?" Her reaction left no doubt as to her position, but it took me completely by surprise. She hadn't found a job in the short time we had been in the D.C. area, but I thought that, like me, she had enjoyed our new home in North Bethesda and exploring the area on weekends.

"Really?"

"Yes," she said. "I'm ready to go back to Atlanta. I wasn't going to tell you how hard this move has been, but this seems to be my cue. I want to go back." For her it was an answer to prayer.

I followed up with Mayor Reed, telling him I was open to returning to Atlanta, but on one condition—that I would be offered the job only after a nationwide posting that also gave senior officers in Atlanta a shot. Having helped establish the department as an "-ism-free" organization in its operational doctrine and pushed for better opportunities for in-house advancement, I felt that every member interested in the position deserved a chance to compete for the appointment.

During the selection process, I came to see the wisdom in how God had nudged me to contact the three main mayoral contenders when I was contemplating the move to D.C. The first phase of interview questions regarding my potential return to Atlanta was a citizens' review panel. I was able to tell them about introducing the AFRD Doctrine and my efforts in championing nondiscrimination. The panel asked many challenging but fair questions, to which I was able to give answers based on data and procedures that seemed to satisfy them.

The final question was the toughest: There was some negative chatter in the department about my coming back, the panelists said. Some of the staff thought I'd used Atlanta as a stepping stone to the U.S. Fire Administration, and now because I couldn't cut it or didn't like it in the capital, I wanted my old position back. There was an erosion of trust.

"Those are legitimate concerns, but the rumors are false," I answered calmly. I went on to explain how my heart was knitted to Atlanta and I had been hoping to stay, but my future there was not certain when I was approached about the federal position. I explained how I had decided to contact the three mayoral candidates to see if they could assure me of a job in their new administration.

I told how I had tried but failed to connect with Mayor Reed but had spoken to the two others—one of whom was now chairing that very panel I was in front of at that moment. That person could vouch for what I said. "Isn't that true?" I asked.

"Yes," she said. "That's correct."

The second phase of the process included a community leadership panel. I answered all its questions satisfactorily, and then the topic of my moves between Shreveport, Atlanta, and Washington, D.C., was raised. This panel was chaired by the other mayoral candidate I had spoken with—the one who had asked to provide a higher public profile for her friend, who was now competing for my vacated position. She too had no option but to confirm what I had said about trying to stay in Atlanta.

I also had to deal with questions over leaving the U.S. fire administrator role so soon—but this time, the question came from an unlikely source—me. While I knew God sometimes calls us to do things that don't seem to make much sense, and though I discerned His hand in all of it, I was still a little uneasy. My high commitment to sacrifice and service made me wonder whether I was being disloyal to President Obama. It wasn't typical to walk out on a presidential appointment after such a brief stay.

"God," I prayed, "if it's really You sending me back to Atlanta, then why did You bring me here in the first place?" His immediate response was: *Because you believed I would.*

He reminded me of a Bible passage that had become very meaningful to me when I had started to grow in my relationship with Him. I had been struck by how, when Moses led his people out of slavery in Egypt, he addressed them as they stood on the edge of the Promised Land. In Deuteronomy 28, God declared all the ways He would bless them if they diligently followed His ways. In verse 13, Moses said, "And the Lord shall make thee the head and not the tail; and thou shalt be above only, and thou shalt not be beneath."

That was my confirmation. I sensed God's telling me that in my time serving in the highest fire service position in the nation, He had made me the head, just as He had promised. And now I could go back to the city to which He also had called me knowing it was not a step back.

Here's what I discovered: when you are walking in obedience, whatever the next assignment God has for your life might be, it's always a promotion, no matter what the world may think.

Still, it wasn't an easy conversation with my superiors at FEMA. Thankfully, they were understanding, and soon I was released. Ironically, I would not actually meet President Obama—whom I had been so proud to serve—in person until a few months after I had returned to Atlanta. While I was still serving in the capital, Carolyn and I had been scheduled to attend a bowling night with other presidential appointees and the Obamas at the White House, but the event had to be canceled because of "Snowmageddon"—a winter storm that temporarily paralyzed the city. When I did eventually get to shake the president's hand, it was in my capacity as Atlanta's fire chief when he visited the city soon after my return.

■   ■   ■

Having won over those in the hiring process who questioned whether I should return to Atlanta, I knew that I had to do the same within the department. I tackled the issue head-on in my first meeting with all the chief officers when I reviewed our organizational structure and leadership values. As part of my presentation, I included a slide listing the mistakes I had made in my first go-round as fire chief. I wanted my leadership team to know that I'd been reflecting during my time away and wanted to model the kind of honesty and humility I was looking for from them.

Among the errors I admitted to making were not always holding chief officers accountable to agreed-upon performance standards and failing to implement the findings of an investigation into the death of a firefighter who had died in the line of duty prior to my arrival in Atlanta the first time. That investigation had revealed that the department needed to make changes in training and practices to avoid a similar tragedy, but we had not implemented all of them.

In one way, some of those dropped balls were understandable. It was an incredibly busy first year or so spent coping with all the budget cuts. Plus, it's not wise to go in waving a big stick at everything as the new boss. That only creates resistance. Transformational leaders always prioritize the changes they want to introduce to avoid overwhelming the team.

Still, even if my failings during my first tenure were explainable, they were not excusable, and I wanted to own them publicly, believing that people are more likely to trust someone who admits they don't always get it right than someone who pretends they never do anything wrong.

Being willing to acknowledge your mistakes is crucial, because only then are you really open to learning how to avoid repeating them; otherwise, you are too busy trying to cover your tracks to be teachable. That was why I had instituted an unusual policy when I first arrived in Atlanta: if an investigation revealed a member of the department had failed in some way, and if that person accepted responsibility for his or her actions, I would always sign off on the lesser of the disciplinary options the review board recommended to me—every time, without fail.

This wasn't about letting people get away with things; it was about helping them learn from mistakes and encouraging a culture of openness to correction. Over time, it won me some appreciation within the department. Most of my disciplinary meetings ended with me shaking hands with the person receiving corrective action.

I didn't always get my way, however. One firefighter suffered serious burns to his hands because he was not wearing his gloves on a call-out—a clear breach of protocol. Some thought he shouldn't be disciplined for it, but to me there was no question. Not only had he been hurt and missed work as a result—costing the city of Atlanta his medical treatment—but his actions might encourage someone else to think they didn't have to wear all the appropriate protective gear. Not only was my disciplinary action in that case unpopular with other firefighters, but the injured man himself appealed my decision to the Civil Service Board, which ruled in his favor.

■   ■   ■

When 2011 rolled around, I started the New Year as I usually did: with a ten-day fast seeking God's wisdom and direction. I explained my practice to Mayor Reed and to Police Chief
George Turner and Patrick Labat, the chief of the Department
of Corrections—the three men with whom I shared responsibility for the safety of the city—and invited them to join me. They
all agreed.

By this time, I had learned that Mayor Reed had something
of a reputation for being a little ornery at times—the *Atlanta
Journal-Constitution* would in due course note his tendency to
"get testy"—and I began to see glimpses of that. He didn't like
it when people disagreed with him. I was also surprised to hear
him using profanity casually when women were around. That
was certainly not the way I had been raised, and when I'd developed a bit of a foul mouth as a young firefighter, I had been called
to account about it in no uncertain terms.

Bad language was part of the culture among guys in the
neighborhood and a fire station or two back then, and I had
picked up on it while trying to fit in. I got pretty good at it, to be
honest. Things came to a head one day at Station Nine when we
were playing volleyball, as we would in the evenings to pass the
time and keep fit.

There was still only a handful of female firefighters in the
department, but a nurse who worked at a nearby hospital started
riding out with us to learn about our response to EMS calls. She
was at one volleyball match when I made a particularly impressive

spike that caused me to let loose with a stream of boastful profanity. It was more posturing than anything.

The firehouse captain, whom I admired for his professionalism and experience, called me around the corner for a verbal reprimand—and that's putting it mildly.

"Klein, we've been putting up with you cursing since you've been here," he said. "But today you crossed a line: you cursed in front of a woman. You let that be the last time you ever do that."

"Yes, sir," I answered. And I stopped cursing cold from that day, embarrassed that I had let down one of my heroes.

In addition to Mayor Reed's occasional off-color language, I also discovered his tendency to be somewhat controlling. As part of returning to Atlanta, I'd asked for permission to fulfill some commitments I had already made to speak at fire service conferences, and he had given it. But he must have forgotten this somewhere along the way, because one day I was called to his office for a meeting with him and the city's chief operating officer.

The mayor questioned these speaking trips, challenging my loyalty and commitment to the city of Atlanta. Though chastisement was unjustified, I knew that being argumentative wouldn't help. I just assured him of my absolute commitment to Atlanta and to the welfare of its people, and reminded him that he and the COO had approved the trips I had made. Realizing he had spoken out of turn, Mayor Reed dialed things back, but told me not to book any other travel without his permission.

I remembered that the following Mother's Day. I wanted to go to Shreveport so Carolyn and I could visit our moms. I hadn't taken a vacation since I had been back in Atlanta, so I figured one day wouldn't be a big problem. But when I requested the time off, Mayor Reed said no—he wanted his leaders in the city for the holiday. I didn't press the issue, chalking it up to a little muscle flexing on his behalf.

These incidents were only minor hiccups in what was a good working relationship, for the most part. If things were going well, the way he wanted, Mayor Reed let you get on with your job. And when leading a big city like Atlanta, there was plenty else to keep him busy.

■　　■　　■

Mayor Reed was true to his word in recruiting me. Over the next couple of years, all the fire department programs and positions that had been cut were restored. Additionally, Fire Station Seven—whose closure had been the source of much contention—was reopened. We achieved full staffing for the first time in the department's history and also improved response times throughout the city. In 2012, we met response-time benchmarks set by the National Fire Protection Association 81 percent of the time—up from 65 percent upon my return to Atlanta. Those benchmarks were among the reasons I was named Fire Chief of the Year by *Fire Chief* magazine in 2012, a real honor. The award prompted Mayor Reed to publicly recognize my "pioneering efforts to improve performance and service within the Atlanta Fire Rescue Department."

Even more affirming than his words was receiving the award during the International Association of Fire Chiefs Fire-Rescue International Conference in Denver, Colorado, in front of my peers. To be honored by so many men and woman I considered to be the best in the industry was a really special moment.

We continued to make solid progress in Atlanta. The following year we earned a Class One rating from the Insurance Services Office. Only a small percentage of big cities meets the stringent criteria for that designation, so raising our grade from a Class Three in such a short time was a major achievement. After four years of hard work, Atlanta had become the "safer city" Mayor Reed had sought. Again, he complimented my efforts.

Mayor Reed's profile was rising nationally. He was named one of the ten most influential African Americans in the country by one publication, among the top state and local government officials of 2011 by another. With regular flattering press coverage and media appearances, there was chatter about higher national office one day, after he stepped down as mayor.

In late 2012, Mayor Reed followed in the footsteps of President Obama, with whom he had been compared, by announcing a major change in his views: He came out in support of gay marriage. Some wondered whether this had anything to do with his forthcoming re-election campaign; he had beaten a same-sex marriage champion by just a few hundred votes the first time around, when he only supported civil unions. Public opinion on the issue had shifted even further in favor of the gay lobby since then.

A columnist for the *Atlanta Journal-Constitution* observed that President Obama's "evolution" on same-sex marriage had "condemned" Mayor Reed to "an interesting re-election bid… where victory lies in striking a balance between a sometimes culturally conservative African-American base and an increasingly powerful gay community."

For his part, Mayor Reed denied that his change of heart had anything to do with electioneering. "If I wanted to play politics, I would have done it when I was in third place in the mayoral election [in 2009] and in front of the gay and lesbian community saying I was not supportive of marriage equality," he said. "As a result of that, I suffered great political harm." Rather, he said he had shifted in his position after a long period of personal reflection.

I was not entirely surprised by his reversal, given that the city council had recently passed a resolution in support of gay marriage that required his signature, effectively backing him into a corner. But knowing that he spoke of his Christian faith—his grandfather was a pastor—and sometimes made reference to his faith in God, I wondered how he reconciled his new view with the Bible's clear teaching on marriage as being exclusively between a man and a woman.

This impacted the fire department only slightly, however. Not long after Mayor Reed's change of heart, he sanctioned official fire department participation in Atlanta's large annual gay pride parade. LGBT members of the department had taken part personally in previous years, of course, but for the first time we provided vehicles for the event with the city's stamp of approval.

Meanwhile, we continued to work on restoring and developing services according to the "-ism-free" doctrine we had embraced during my first season in the city. With clear-cut principles and procedures spelled out, personal opinions did not come into play. That was why I took immediate corrective action when some firefighters publicly made anti-gay statements. With same-sex marriage a hot-button topic, one of Atlanta's most successful family-run businesses, Chick-fil-A, had come under attack for supporting traditional marriage, which was in line with its founder's personal beliefs.

That led to an LGBT boycott of the restaurant, and Christians turned out in large numbers to support their local Chick-fil-A locations. While on duty, one of our fire crews went to a nearby Chick-fil-A, and the members posted a photo of themselves eating there on social media, along with a comment about how they supported the business. Another firefighter posted a comment about the photo, using an offensive slur to describe gay people.

This was brought to my attention by a member of the public who called to complain. I assured him that such behavior was against our departmental policies and values and that I would have our internal affairs team investigate.

Whether or not I personally agreed with the firefighters' support of Chick-fil-A was irrelevant: the crew appeared to have violated a clear departmental procedure. Our firefighters could say what they wanted on their own time, as civilians, but to do so and make it seem as though it were somehow endorsed by the department was plain wrong. And for the one who made an offensive comment, there was just no defense. The internal affairs inquiry concluded that both the firefighter who had posted the photo and the one who had commented on it derogatorily had violated department standards, and they were disciplined as a result.

It may not have made me popular with some in the department, but that is always going to be the case in leadership. That is why it is so important to have clear shared values, goals, and standards that eliminate personal preference or prejudice. A safer city must be safe for all its citizens to live out their consciences.

CHAPTER TEN

The Naked Truth

*To everything there is a season and a time for every
purpose under heaven.*

—*Ecclesiastes 3:1 BSB*

B eing back in Atlanta began another season of harvest. At
work, I was seeing the fruit of some of the seeds I had sown
during my first stint there as fire chief with what felt like a new
sense of vision and unity in the department. At home, we were
also enjoying our life together and at Elizabeth Baptist Church,
to which we had returned.

Life in Washington, D.C., had been exciting and fulfilling,
but it never quite felt like home. I respected the men and women
I worked alongside, but there wasn't the same sense of community I had experienced in the fire departments in Shreveport and
Atlanta. Some of that was because a special bond develops when
you are part of a team and putting yourselves on the line together
every day. Some of it was the climate created by the culture of
federal government; there is a measure of competitiveness in

every workplace, of course, but to me it seemed to be heightened in the nation's capital. The core of the fire departments I had known at the local level had been our shared sense of patriotism, despite our differences, and a military-like sense of duty. In the capital, the core driver seemed to be survival and political posturing. Some people were looking more to impress others than to work together.

On top of that was the different lifestyle. Carolyn and I had been used to living in communities where we would share greetings with our neighbors when we saw them in their yards or walking in the neighborhood. In North Bethesda we lived in an apartment building where an exchange of pleasantries with neighbors between the parking garage and the elevator to the seventh floor was uncommon. So we were altogether elated to move back into our old home, which had not sold despite being on the market, and to renew old friendships at Elizabeth Baptist and make new ones.

Not having a position of responsibility, as I had for so long back at our church in Shreveport, meant that Carolyn and I were together more in services and small group studies, which we really enjoyed. Over time, I was asked to contribute to a Sunday school lesson here and there and then became one of the facilitators. Eventually, I was invited to serve as a deacon. One of the responsibilities I most enjoyed was visiting some of the church's home-bound seniors each month to sit and talk, share communion, and hand them a nice new fifty-dollar bill, a little gesture of love and care from the church. In some ways it reminded me of my boyhood days visiting folks to deliver the latest edition of the *Shreveport Sun*.

I also liked taking part in small groups with other guys. From my past struggles, I knew how important it was to be around other men who wanted to follow God faithfully and serve Him well at home and at work. In those connections I had found Proverbs 27:17 to be true: "Iron sharpens iron, and one man sharpens another."

I was asked to help facilitate a men's group studying *The Quest for Authentic Manhood* by Dr. Robert Lewis. Each week we'd watch a video in which he spoke about what the Bible had to say about being a man who walked in God's ways. In the fourth week, while looking at the consequences of Adam's fall in the Garden of Eden, I opened the conversation by asking the guys if they felt they were still dealing with the effects of his failure. They all said yes, sharing about different areas in their lives where they were struggling with issues like sexual purity, pride, anger, or addiction.

What struck me hard was not so much the things they named, but their tone. There was a lot of guilt and shame and condemnation. A sense of resignation that things would never get any better, and this just was the way it was. It seemed a long way from the joy and freedom and victory we sang about in church. Jesus may have said with finality on the cross, "It is finished," but many men seemed to doubt that was true in their lives.

In particular, part of the Bible account we had read stuck with me—when God came to Adam after he and Eve had eaten fruit from the tree of the knowledge of good and evil, despite having been warned not to. In Genesis 3:11, God asked Adam, "Who told you that you were naked?" The question kept running through my head on an endless loop. I felt like God was nudging me to dig deep to find out more, that He had something to say to me—and others.

I began to spend some of my daily morning time with God reading and praying about it. First I zeroed in on the word *naked*. I found every verse in the Bible where it appeared. Then I looked up the definition in Hebrew, the language of the Old Testament—and in Greek, the language of the New Testament. I realized that in the context of the Garden of Eden, *naked* didn't just mean not having any clothes on. More fully, it meant being condemned and deprived. That was what God was asking Adam: "Who told you that you are condemned and deprived?"

Next I turned to the word *clothed*, following the same process. After they had eaten the forbidden fruit, Adam and Eve had tried to cover themselves with fig leaves, but their efforts were not enough: God made garments of skin for them (Genesis 3:21). After studying all the references, I came to the conclusion that God wasn't just speaking about not having pants on. In the context of the Garden of Eden, being *clothed* meant being redeemed and restored. I was excited by what I had found. God wasn't speaking about Adam's surface in asking, "Who told you that you were naked?" He was talking about what was going on deep inside.

Having begun writing in my journal, I switched to my computer as my research continued. By the time I had finished, I had more than thirty pages of notes. *That's almost enough for a book*, I thought, though not seriously.

What I learned made an impact on me. I'd pursued God diligently for many years by then. I was confident that I had been forgiven for all of the many mistakes I had made in my life—at least, most of the time. To be honest, there were still occasions when I would find myself laboring under a heaviness over some misstep. My studies on nakedness and clothing made me aware in a new way of the completeness of salvation: Because of Jesus's death and resurrection, we can stand before God knowing we are forgiven and accepted. What Jesus did on the cross was greater than what Adam did in the Garden of Eden! Really grasping this was so liberating. I had a greater sense of freedom in knowing that God no longer saw me as a sinner. Yes, I still sinned from time to time, but those were my actions—not my identity.

I was curious to see whether this message would resonate with other men. I asked a group of guys I met with each Friday morning at Q-Time Restaurant on the city's west side—we called ourselves the Urban Christian Network—if they'd like to hear some of what I had found. They agreed, and over the course of six weeks I saw lights go on for some of the others, just as they had for me, as I spoke about the full and true freedom God had in store for us in and through Jesus.

I sensed that more guys like us—and maybe a few women reading over their shoulders—might benefit from what I had found. I was willing to speak whenever and wherever I was given the opportunity, but I already had a full-time job. Maybe if I put it all into a book, I could reach some more people with some encouragement. The friends I had shared the material with encouraged me to do so.

Over the next several months, I took my research and notes and developed them. When I had finished my manuscript, I took it to 3G Publishing, which was not far away in Loganville, Geor-gia. I asked for an initial print run of five hundred copies, which seemed like a lot but helped reduce my costs. I thought I might sell through them over time, as I got to speak at different churches. And I knew that God could do more than we might envision or imagine.

"God, open a way for this book, please," I prayed as I held my first copy in December 2013. "I want to share this word all over the world."

■   ■   ■

Knowing that firefighters' having other jobs was a part of the department's culture, and because I had written the book entirely on my own time, I was confident that I was not violating any employment policies. But as I finished the manuscript, I decided to double-check with the city's ethics officer.

I called and told her I was working on a faith-based book that had nothing to do with the fire department. I told her the title and explained the theme—helping men overcome condem-nation. She said it sounded interesting and that she would like a copy when it was finished. As long as it had nothing to do with the fire department or city government, she said, there was noth-ing to prevent me from publishing a book like that. Some months later, as I neared completion, I called again: Would there be any problem with my mentioning in my bio in the book that I was the Atlanta fire chief? No, she told me.

It's a sad reflection of the times that speaking directly to some-one can be seen as trying to be evasive, rather than effective.

However, in hindsight, much of what followed might have been averted if I had sent an email rather than called. There would have been a clear "paper trail" to prove my case. But I wasn't thinking defensively—there seemed to be no reason to do so—and it was often quicker to get things done by picking up the phone or walking down the hall and seeing someone in person rather than adding to their email inbox.

I'd experienced that before. Once, a situation had blown up at the training academy: some of the female cadets had been shocked when another trainee with male genitalia used their locker room. This was before transsexual issues became more commonplace, and it caused quite a stir. It turned out that the person concerned was a female pseudohermaphrodite—a biological woman with male genitalia. The situation needed a quick response, so I called the city's human resources director for some immediate guidance. Following her advice, I was able to ensure we followed the correct procedures for all involved so the issue was dealt with quickly and appropriately. There wasn't time to sit around and exchange emails; those kinds of fires need to be put out before they get out of control.

The biographical reference in my manuscript was innocuous; it merely noted that I was "currently serving as Fire Chief of the City of Atlanta Fire Rescue Department." There was one mention of my position in the actual text, in a passage where I explained how, just as Adam was placed in the Garden of Eden to cultivate and keep it, men had been given a similar role. I wrote:

> Personal Life Application: God gave me my fire service
> land, field, career. He gave me the job of being a fire

service leader, Fire Chief of Atlanta Fire Rescue. He also made me the head—United States Fire Administrator. My job description as a fire chief of Atlanta Fire Rescue Department is: To cultivate its culture for the glory of God. To keep it focused on its mission of saving lives and property. To sustain its culture, its members and its capabilities, both now and for future generations.

My point was that the same is true for every man—he has a God-given assignment and purpose to fulfill in his life and work.

The word *homosexuality* appeared just once in what I had written, in a section about the seventeen "works of the flesh" described in Galatians 5:19–21. I wrote, "Uncleanness—whatever is opposite of purity; including sodomy, homosexuality, lesbianism, pederasty, bestiality, and all other forms of sexual perversion." I did refer to homosexuality in a couple of other places, noting that God intended sex to be between a man and a woman, and that "naked men"—meaning those who have not been "clothed" in Christ through salvation—"refuse to give in, so they pursue sexual fulfillment through multiple partners, with the opposite sex, same sex and sex outside of marriage and many other vile, vulgar and inappropriate ways which defile their body-temple and dishonor God."

In another section, I distinguished the different ways in which God views men who are "clothed" (walking according to His ways) from those who are "naked" (not walking according to His ways). I quoted thirty-two verses from Proverbs, in each one using *naked* or *clothed* in place of whatever synonym was there.

Included was Proverbs 11:10: "When it goes well with the clothed the city rejoices; when the naked perish there is shouting." (I would later be accused of using this passage to show hatefulness toward the LGBT community.)

Nowhere in my writing did I offer a personal opinion or commentary. I based everything I said on what I found in Scripture, knowing that only it had the power to make an impact. I wasn't trying to change readers' minds by what I said. I wanted their hearts to be changed by what God said. I wanted them to really, truly grasp the liberty that was theirs through Jesus. I believed that when men rose up to be all that God called them to be, confident in His forgiveness and grace, we would start to see real revival. I wanted to start a spiritual fire.

When the book came out, I gave a few copies to a handful of guys in the department. Six went to people who had asked me for one when I'd mentioned what I was working on. I gave another three, unsolicited, to guys I knew to be men of faith from previous interactions. One of them was a Methodist preacher. I also gave a copy each to a couple of members of the city council whom I knew to be Christians.

I wanted to let Mayor Reed have a signed copy, as well, so I took one along to a reception for the person who was going to be taking over as Atlanta's COO. Mayor Reed didn't show at the event, so I gave the book to his executive assistant, who promised to make sure he got it.

When I saw Mayor Reed a day or so later at the annual State of the City Breakfast, I asked him about the book. Yes, he had received it, he said. He quoted the title and told me he planned to read it on a forthcoming trip to China.

■   ■   ■

As I said earlier, to start a fire you need three things: oxygen, fuel, and ignition. I wasn't aware that *Who Told You That You Were Naked?* would be the fuel for my personal firestorm, nor how much the temperature of the cultural atmosphere had been quietly rising toward a flashpoint since I had returned to Atlanta.

It had escaped my attention that just a few months before I returned from D.C., Atlanta was named the "Gayest City in America" by *The Advocate*, a magazine dedicated to the LGBT lifestyle. The designation was based on the number of same-sex households per capita, the number of gay elected officials, gay dating profiles, and other criteria. "With 29 gay bars here, there's a reason it's dubbed Hotlanta," correspondent Mike Albo wrote. He also cited Atlanta's hosting one of the largest gay pride events in the country, its large gay bookstore, and "seriously well organized" gay sports leagues for its top spot in the list.

While this ranking may not have been based on the strictest criteria, it did reflect what was happening in the city. According to the 2010 U.S. Census, Atlanta ranked sixth nationwide among cities for its percentage of same-sex couples, behind Berkeley, Oakland, and San Francisco in California, then Seattle and Fort Lauderdale. It is also worth noting that around the time I published my book, Mayor Reed, who had won his first mayoral race by a slim margin, had been returned to office with strong support from the gay community following his reversal on the issue of same-sex marriage.

Only later did I learn who struck the match that started my career-ending fire. One of the people to whom I had given a copy of the book was a senior officer I'd demoted for failing to meet the standards required of the position. Though I considered him a brother in Christ, I'd not allowed that to sway me from clear departmental policies.

This senior officer took a copy of the book to the president of the Atlanta Professional Fire Fighters Union. Fire service culture historically suggests that management and union reps are supposed to be at odds with each other. But while we'd had our different priorities and disagreements through the years, naturally, our relationship had always been cordial and professional. I knew this union rep and I shared the same faith; indeed, at one stage I had been able to offer him some personal encouragement and advice when he was facing challenges in his personal life.

Having received a copy of the book from the senior officer I had demoted, the union rep felt he should bring it to the attention of Alex Wan, an openly gay council member. Wan had sponsored the 2010 city resolution that had prompted Mayor Reed to openly reverse his position on same-sex issues. I'd never had any problems with Wan, who always seemed friendly and diligent in serving his constituents. The last time we had met was just a couple or so weeks before things blew up, at a memorial service for a member of the city administration who had lost a newborn. We spent some time there talking easily together about plans to upgrade a fire station in his district.

My book had been available for ten months by then without any negative reaction. I had sold only a handful of copies online, and some at a couple of speaking engagements. In fact, the weekend before I was suspended, I had traveled to my old church in Shreveport to share the message in person and sell some copies. I had returned to Atlanta encouraged by how it had been received.

So I wasn't too concerned even when I received calls from some friends in the city government giving me the heads-up that there might be a problem with the book. I figured that even if someone was trying to make it an issue, the whole thing would blow over pretty quickly. Even if Mayor Reed didn't agree with my position, I was confident that he would defend my right to express it as I had, on my own time. The last time he and I had been in direct contact had been just a few weeks earlier, at the beginning of November, when we learned that Atlanta had earned its Class One insurance rating. He had texted me congratulations, saying it was the best news he'd received since the birth of his daughter a few months earlier.

Having served city governments for so many years, I had learned to read a room. So I could tell things were serious when I got to the meeting with Mayor Reed's chief of staff, the commissioner of human resources, and one of the city's attorneys. There was a slight tension in the air, a formality that set the tone for what was to come.

Someone had done his or her homework. There was a copy of my book on the desk with the "problem" portions underscored. I was told that Mayor Reed did not agree with some of what I had said in the book and that it had offended members of the LGBT community. I was being suspended without pay for thirty days, effective immediately. I was to conduct no media interviews. There would be an investigation, and I'd need to undergo sensitivity training before I returned to duty. No one cited any specific policy I was alleged to have violated.

Although I was disappointed by the news, I wasn't unduly worried. I was confident that any thorough review would exonerate me of all wrongdoing. I told them I'd cooperate with their actions. "I'll do the sensitivity training, too," I said, "but to be honest I don't see how that's going to help. This is what I believe God says, and I don't see sensitivity training changing that."

The first call I took after leaving the meeting with the three city representatives was from Pastor Oliver at Elizabeth Baptist. Clearly, word was getting around the city fast. I was touched by his concern, but told him I was okay. When I explained the background of the story, he assured me the church would stand with me all the way.

Another sign of the speed with which the news was spreading came after I got home to an empty house; Carolyn was still at work. The doorbell rang, and there was a reporter from one of the local television news stations, wondering whether I had anything to say. I explained that I was not in a position to speak to the media.

According to the *Atlanta Journal-Constitution*, Mayor Reed's office said I "was not available for interviews." However, while I honored my commitment to media silence, the city was quick to present its version of events. In a press statement that afternoon announcing my suspension, Mayor Reed said, "I want to be clear that the material in Chief Cochran's book is not representative of my personal beliefs and is inconsistent with the administration's work to make Atlanta a more welcoming city for all of her citizens—regardless of their sexual orientation, gender, race, and religious beliefs."

Carolyn was upset when she got home and learned what had happened, but my sense of calm seemed to reassure her. I called each of our children, my mom, and our former pastor in Shreveport so they could learn about the situation from me directly instead of the evening news. I told them not to worry, God was in this, and I was trusting Him to see me through. The situation felt similar to what had happened when that community hall roof had collapsed on Don and me. But in spite of it all, I was confident that if I kept calm and stayed on my knees, I could come through this fire unscathed.

CHAPTER ELEVEN

Faith amid the Flames

*Shadrach, Meshach, and Abednego answered and said
to the king, O Nebuchadnezzer, we are not careful to
answer thee in this matter. If it be so, our God whom
we serve is able to deliver us from the burning fiery furnace, and he will deliver us out of thine hand, O king.*

—Daniel 3:16–17 KJV

Since I'd been instructed to stay away from the fire department, I enjoyed Thanksgiving with Carolyn in Shreveport as
we visited our moms—a rare family celebration. Old friends
back there had heard about my suspension and were encouraging, applauding me for standing strong in my faith.

As word started to spread, what the city had tried to position
as a stand for tolerance on its part was being seen by many as
the exact opposite—something that actually cut across constitutional rights. Councilman Wan may not have realized the full
magnitude of what he was saying when he told the *Atlanta
Journal-Constitution* that he respected an individual's rights to
have his own thoughts, beliefs, and opinions, "but when you're
a city employee, and those thoughts, beliefs, and opinions are
different from the city's, you have to check them at the door."

Not only did that fly in the face of the Constitution's bedrock principle of religious liberty, but it was also illogical. When I had been hired as Atlanta's fire chief, Mayor Reed had not been a supporter of same-sex marriage; we had shared a similar perspective. By Councilman Wan's reasoning, that should have meant that people who were advocates of same-sex marriage shouldn't have been free to express their views at the time—but they were, and they did, without any suggestion of censure. And rightly so. Were city workers supposed to check the administration's policy each day, like the weather, to see whether they were still "in step," or if something had changed?

While I honored my agreement not to speak to the media, the city kept spinning the situation. At one stage, Mayor Reed's spokesperson said the administration hadn't known about my book until employees came forward with complaints directly before my suspension. That was simply false; not only had I talked with the city's ethics officer, but Mayor Reed himself had quoted the title of the book to me personally.

While we were in Shreveport, I received a call from an unknown number. The caller was a man named Ed Setzler. He introduced himself as a Georgia state legislator; I knew of him, but we had never had any direct contact. He told me he wasn't contacting me in that capacity, but as a brother in Christ. He and some other state legislators had heard of my story and were praying for me, he said.

It was so encouraging to get an unsolicited message of support like that. Setzler went on to give me a list of people he said it might be helpful for me to contact. I scribbled down the details and thanked him, though I wasn't sure I would need them. I was still of a mind that when the inquiry cleared me of any wrongdoing, everything would blow over and I would be back at my desk early in the new year.

Still, I felt it would be courteous to at least to call some of the people the senator had suggested. One of them was Jonathan Crumly, an attorney in Atlanta who told me he did some work with Alliance Defending Freedom (ADF), a Christian-based legal organization that represents believers caught in religious-liberty cases like mine pro bono. I ended up meeting with him and Garland Hunt, another Atlanta-area attorney with links to ADF; Garland also pastored a church in the area.

They affirmed me for the stand I had taken and told me how ADF could help me carry the weight of the legal and financial pressure brought by the city of Atlanta, as it had helped other Christians caught in the crosshairs of religious persecution. Most everyday believers had neither the legal background nor the deep pockets it takes to challenge government or big business, they explained. I listened and told them I appreciated their concern, but in reality, I was kind of dismissive. I was sure I would soon be exonerated.

One of the other names on Setzler's list was Mike Griffin, the public affairs officer for the Georgia Baptist Mission Board. He told me he knew I couldn't speak to the press, but he asked if I could speak at an executive committee meeting of the board. There didn't seem to be anything to prevent me from doing that, so I went to the group's offices in Duluth, where I was introduced to a couple hundred pastors from across the state.

I told my story about growing up poor and fatherless and my childhood dream of becoming a firefighter. I described some of the prejudice I had faced as I rose through the ranks and how God had blessed me beyond my wildest dreams as I committed to living according to His ways. I explained how I had come to write my book and how the city had handled things. I made sure not to speak ill of anyone, always referring respectfully to "the Honorable Mayor, Kasim Reed."

I took this cue from the lives of David, Shadrach, Meshach, and Abednego. David did not lift a hand against King Saul when he had the opportunity to do so. "Don't destroy him! Who can lay a hand on the Lord's anointed and be guiltless?" he said to those who suggested he take advantage of the moment to clear his way to the throne (1 Samuel 26:9). Even as Shadrach, Meshach, and Abednego defied King Nebuchadnezzar's edict to bow down before a golden idol, they did so respectfully, addressing him as "O king" (Daniel 3:17–18 KJV).

I told the Baptist gathering that I wasn't afraid or discouraged by what had happened, that I believed God had been preparing me for this challenge all my life, and that He would see me through.

I closed by reciting one of my favorite passages of Scripture, Psalm 27:

> The Lord is my light and my salvation—whom shall I fear? The Lord is the stronghold of my life—of whom shall I be afraid? When the wicked advance against me to devour me, it is my enemies and my foes who will stumble and fall.... For in the day of trouble he will keep me safe in his dwelling; he will hide me in the shelter of his sacred tent and set me high upon a

rock. Then my head will be exalted above the enemies who surround me.... I remain confident of this: I will see the goodness of the Lord in the land of the living. Wait for the Lord; be strong and take heart and wait for the Lord.

Mike had asked me to take some copies of my book along with me on my trip, so I did—and I ended up selling more than I had in the year-plus since its publication. Like splashing gasoline on an open fire, the city's action in seeking to punish me for what I had written had only served to fan the flames and promote the message. I took it as another sign that God was with me in everything that was happening and He would somehow use it all to His ends.

My visit had another unexpected result: The convention launched an online petition calling on Mayor Reed to apologize to me for ignoring my First Amendment rights and restore my pay and reputation. They also urged people to buy my book and encouraged them to support me by writing to Mayor Reed to protest—citing his email and mailing address in a Baptist press release about my appearance at the convention. That was a little awkward, but it was beyond my control—I'd kept my word about not speaking directly to the media. I called the city's chief operating officer to assure him that I hadn't been party to the decision to publicize my visit with the mission board.

Mayor Reed wasn't happy, however. He ended up receiving hundreds of emails and letters supporting me, "even thousands," according to the *Atlanta Journal-Constitution.* Some people sent him Bibles, while others called him the anti-Christ. I didn't condone any of the unkind words, but I did appreciate that so many people voiced their support for me. Mayor Reed couldn't help but hear that while some of his constituents may have supported his actions, they certainly were not popular universally.

▪   ▪   ▪

As Christmas loomed without a paycheck, Carolyn suggested that we trim back our usual holiday plans, but I felt that we should carry on as usual and trust God to provide. He did. And I made the most of my free time. Each morning I'd get up early as usual and spend extended time with God on my own, with no need to watch the clock. My journals filled with promises of His faithfulness. Then I'd spend the rest of the morning working on my ongoing doctorate studies in leadership through Creighton University. After lunch I would exercise, taking long walks and bike rides. Then I'd kick back and watch some old TV shows from my youth: *The Andy Griffith Show*, of course, and also *Bonanza* and *Gunsmoke*. There was something comforting about them, taking me back to a time when I knew God was watching over me as a boy, even if I didn't know what lay ahead.

There was just one day when I was tempted to give way to despair and doubt. It was after the holidays, and Carolyn had returned to work and the kids were gone. I felt a wave of uncertainty washing up against me and rising around me. Maybe the situation I was in was punishment for all my past wrongs? Just when it seemed as though I'd drown in the heaviness, a portion of Scripture came to mind. Rather than hold my breath as I was submerged by hopelessness, I spoke out some of the words of King David:

> Lift up your heads, you gates; be lifted up, you ancient doors, that the King of glory may come in. Who is this King of glory? The Lord strong and mighty, the Lord mighty in battle. Lift up your heads, you gates; lift them up, you ancient doors, that the King of glory may come in. Who is he, this King of glory? The Lord Almighty—he is the King of glory. (Psalm 24:7–10)

As I spoke, the sense of dread just drained away, like a grate had opened up under my feet. In its place were peace, faith, and hope once more.

My confidence was boosted by all the support I was receiving. Not that everyone was positive—some death threats were called in for me at the fire department office, I was told. However, for the most part I heard good things. I handled a lot of mail and phone calls from people telling me they were standing with me. Dan Cathy, the CEO of Chick-fil-A, called to say he was praying for me and to let him know if he could help in any way. Franklin Graham, president of the Billy Graham Evangelistic Association, did the same; we had met when I had chaired the committee for the Ark-La-Tex Franklin Graham Festival while in Shreveport ten years or so earlier. When he saw my name in the news, he tracked me down to pledge his help. Ronnie Floyd, the president of the Southern Baptist Convention, also called to offer his support.

Then there were invitations from Baptist churches across the state to share my story. For the next six months, I would be in a different church every Sunday—sometimes two—where people would encourage me to stand strong, pray for me, and give me a love offering. As with my appearance at the Georgia Baptist Mission Board, I always made a point to simply tell what had happened and never to speak negatively of Mayor Reed or the city.

I felt led to do more than just recite what had happened, however. Increasingly aware of the way our national culture was drifting and that Christians were becoming increasingly likely to find themselves targeted for holding to biblical values, I sensed that I had an opportunity and a responsibility to give some guidance and encouragement to others who might experience similar difficulties. It was like being a firefighting training officer again, preparing others to safely face the flames.

I titled my message "The Blessings of Suffering" and began it by quoting 1 Peter 4:12–14:

> Dear friends, do not be surprised at the fiery ordeal that has come on you to test you, as though something strange were happening to you. But rejoice inasmuch as you participate in the sufferings of Christ, so that you may be overjoyed when his glory is revealed. If you are insulted because of the name of Christ, you are blessed, for the Spirit of glory and of God rests on you.

Then I would go on to offer five truths for people to hold on to when they found themselves facing difficulties. First, God always prepares His sons and daughters for suffering—always.

We would not be going through the situation unless God had determined that we were prepared for it, through all that had happened in our lives up to that point.

Second, there are worldly consequences for standing on biblical truth and standing for Christ. That's an unavoidable reality; there is a price to pay for following Jesus in a world that does not recognize Him. Third, however, there are Kingdom benefits for standing on biblical truth and standing for Christ—and these Kingdom benefits are always greater than the worldly consequences. We can never give up more than Jesus promised to restore to us. When Peter told Jesus that he and the disciples had left everything to follow Him, Jesus replied that "everyone who has left houses or brothers or sisters or father or mother or wife or children or fields for my sake will receive a hundred times as much and will inherit eternal life" (Matthew 19:29).

Fourth, while there are two types of suffering—that which is God-allowed and that which we inflict on ourselves by our own poor choices, such as I had suffered in the past—all can bring glory to God. He is always glorified when His sons and daughters endure suffering. Fifth, the life of blessing for those who have the courage and faith to stand for God in the face of suffering will go to a level that is exceedingly, abundantly above all they could ever ask or think.

■   ■   ■

I didn't hear much from the fire department or city government during my suspension, which wasn't too surprising. I knew that anyone who publicly aligned themselves with me in any way would be inviting scrutiny. So I was very grateful for the few people who did reach out to me.

I received a call from the Atlanta police chief, just checking in on me. We had a warm working relationship, not only as the leaders of two of the departments entrusted with Atlantans' safety, but as men of faith. He was one of those who had called to give me the heads-up that trouble was brewing over my book before my suspension.

A senior member of the city council who has since passed away called to say that he did not agree with what had happened to me. Another leading member stopped me when we passed one day to ask how I was doing. She didn't take a side on things, but I appreciated her gesture of concern.

About midway through my suspension, a city commissioner brought a basket of goodies and told me that folks in the office were thinking of me. It was a thoughtful touch that made me wonder whether it might be some sort of coded message from the mayor, maybe saying that he had to do things the way he did but they would all work out. That did not prove to be the case.

One of the city's attorneys was as helpful as he could be when I called to inquire about how the investigation was going. He couldn't go into lots of details, of course, but he did tell me a couple of things. The city's ethics officer disputed saying it was okay for me to write my book, but her notes of our conversation were not definitive. And none of the three people I'd given unsolicited copies of the book to had been offended by it. I took the attorney's courtesy calls as an indication of some sympathy for me.

Given all that, I was quietly confident that everything would be resolved once my thirty days were up and that I would be able to return to duty. I declined ADF's offer to have an attorney accompany me to my post-suspension meeting for two reasons: I was concerned that arriving with a lawyer by my side would look combative, maybe even seen as an admission of wrongdoing. And I thought I would be reinstated.

Initially, I felt confident as I met with the mayor's chief of staff, the commissioner of human resources, and one of the city's attorneys on Monday, January 6, 2015. Though we were sitting on different sides of an issue now, we shared a collaborative past, having worked alongside each other in some difficult situations as members of the cabinet. I was fond of them; I've always believed that you can't have strong working relationships without some measure of emotional investment. We might be professionals, but we are also human beings.

They told me that the investigation had found no evidence of my having treated anyone in the department unfairly or improperly. However, they said, I'd not gotten permission from Mayor Reed to write my book, nor did the city's ethics officer approve it. And what I'd written had offended the LGBT community.

I wouldn't get to see a copy of the City of Atlanta Law Department's four-page report, titled "Investigative Report: Atlanta Fire Rescue Department – Chief Cochran Book Publication," until some days later. It revealed no evidence of any bias:

- "No indication that Chief Cochran allowed his religious beliefs to compromise his disciplinary decisions."
- "No interviewed witness could point to a specific instance in which any member of the organization

has been treated unfairly by Chief Cochran on the basis of his religious beliefs."

- The union leader interviewed "was unable to offer any examples of maltreatment."
- Two retired firefighters interviewed at the suggestion of Mayor Reed's LGBT advisor were "intensely offended by the viewpoints expressed in Chief Cochran's book, but neither provided any examples of having experienced Chief Cochran displaying the influence of any of these viewpoints in his professional capacity."

Despite these specifics refuting the suggestion that I had in any way been unfair, the report also said there was "a consistent sentiment among the witnesses that firefighters throughout the organization are appalled by the sentiments expressed in the book. There also is general agreement the contents of the book have eroded trust and have compromised the ability of the chief to provide leadership in the future." In other words, although there wasn't a shred of evidence from my history that my faith had in any way caused me to treat anyone unfairly, the suggestion was that in the future I might do so.

The meeting with the city's three representatives didn't last long. I reiterated that I believed the ethics officer had cleared me to write the book. I also corrected a claim made in the meeting that I had defied Mayor Reed's directions by speaking to the media during my suspension. I explained that my address to pastors at the Georgia Baptist Mission Board had been reported, but that had been beyond my control and I had not had any direct contact with the media, as I had agreed.

I was presented with a simple option: resign or be fired. Resignation was naturally out of the question for me—to step down would be a tacit admission of guilt on my part and also preclude me from appealing the action. "I'm not going to resign," I told them. "If I had done anything that had gone against policies or procedures in any way and you had evidence, then certainly I would resign. But your own report has exonerated me. There's no way I am going to resign." I asked to meet with Mayor Reed, but I was told that was not an option. I knew then I was on my way out.

I left carrying a copy of the letter terminating my appointment as fire chief. By the time I got back to my office, word had already gotten around. In fact, the city had already released a statement announcing my firing.

I was accompanied to my office by someone from HR. At my desk I plugged a thumb drive into my computer. On it was a draft statement I had prepared in anticipation of my return to duty at the end of my thirty-day suspension. I'd thought it would be easier to handle any media inquiries all in one go with a prepared statement, rather than individual interviews. Clearly, those words needed some revision.

Having reworked them, I contacted the fire department's public information officer to schedule a time for a press conference. "I'm sorry, Chief," he said. "The mayor's office of communication told me to give no support or help with any communication to you for any media. I apologize, but you're on your own." Additionally, he told me I couldn't use the conference room.

I met with the band of journalists waiting outside the Public Safety Headquarters building. I explained how I came to write the book and my record of fairness within the fire department. LGBT members of the community deserved the right to express their beliefs regarding sexual orientation without hate and discrimination, I said—and so did Christians.

"I am not apologetic for writing the book," I said. "I believe that, for Christian men to be all that God has called us to be, we have to overcome a stronghold of condemnation. Everything I wrote in the book is based on Scripture, not opinion." I spoke about how Atlanta had been known from the 1960s as "the city too busy to hate." As fire chief, I said, I had been the same, treating people fairly and equitably.

My office staff waited awkwardly as I boxed up my things. I thanked them for their service and assured them that everything was going to be fine. "Just stand still and see the salvation of God," I told them as I left.

I arrived at an empty house; Carolyn was still at work. As I changed, I knew I was stepping out of my firefighter's uniform for the last time. For thirty-four years I had worn it with pride, but I had no doubt at that moment that my career was over. No city would hire someone with the sort of controversy I had swirling around me.

While I was somewhat saddened, I was not dismayed. I knew I was not at the mercy of men. Everything I had experienced had prepared me for this situation. God was in the middle of this and would work through all that was happening if I trusted Him, just as He had through all my life to that point.

CHAPTER TWELVE

A Time to Stand

*Beloved, think it not strange concerning the fiery trial
which is to try you, as though some strange thing happened to you. But rejoice, inasmuch as ye are partak-
ers of Christ's sufferings; that, when his glory shall be
revealed, ye may be glad also with exceeding joy. If ye
be reproached for the name of Christ, happy are ye; for
the spirit of glory and of God resteth upon you: on their
part he is evil spoken of, but on your part he is glorified.*

—*1 Peter 4:12–14 KJV*

I have never been a gambling man, but I am grateful for one
piece of wisdom from card players: that you have to know
when to hold them, when to fold them, and when to walk away.
This principle guided me through my firefighting career as I
learned when to let things go and when to take a stand. My firing was a time to take a stand.

There were three reasons. First, my reputation had been
impugned. For all that I had done to ensure there was a place for
everyone in the fire department, I had been characterized as a
bigot and a hatemonger. That was simply untrue. I held no animosity toward the LGBT community; I had family members and

peers in the fire service who were openly gay with whom I had warm relationships. I might not agree with their lifestyle, but it didn't affect the way I treated them. Far from "hating" them, I loved them and wanted the best for them.

While it was hurtful personally to be accused of being a homophobe, of course, that wasn't the main impetus for my wanting to confront those claims. It was because I knew what was really at stake was not my reputation but Jesus's. Those who criticize Christians for holding to biblical values are really criticizing the One they follow.

Then, in addition to the professional damage that had been done to me, there was the financial impact. I'd enjoyed a good life as a result of my successful career, but those days were over. By firing me the way he did, Mayor Reed hadn't only ended my Atlanta firefighting career; he had made it impossible for me to find a new position commensurate with my experience. Who would want to hire the guy who got canned for being "hateful"?

Most importantly, however, my termination had not only impacted my life; it had served as a warning shot for any Christian in public service—follow Jesus openly at your peril. In the words of Councilman Wan: you need to check your faith at the door when you get to work. If you hold some sort of significant position, you can't express biblical views in any kind of public forum because someone might get upset. In other words, serving your community during the week means you can't serve as a Sunday school teacher over the weekend? This dangerous idea couldn't go unchallenged.

Actually, far from being a detriment, my faith was a benefit to my public service. It motivated me to love everyone as people made in God's image and to seek the best for them regardless of their religious affiliation, their political persuasion, or their sexual inclination. My faith had also inspired me to become the best firefighter I could be and work hard to improve myself. We had made tremendous strides in the fire department during my years in Atlanta, and I had received several accolades, but I knew those achievements weren't simply because of my efforts; they were a sign of God's blessing as I sought to cultivate the department to His glory.

In fact, I viewed the Preamble of the Constitution as another way of expressing the biblical mandate given to Adam and Eve in the Garden of Eden, to rule and reign over God's creation:

> We the People of the United States, in Order to form a more perfect Union, establish Justice, insure domestic Tranquility, provide for the common defense, promote the general Welfare, and secure the Blessings of Liberty to ourselves and our Posterity, do ordain and establish this Constitution for the United States of America.

Equality, justice, peace, protection of and care for others, freedom—if these are not biblical precepts, I don't know what are. I was also part of a long line of people in public service who openly acknowledged their faith. Both times that I had become fire chief, in Shreveport and Atlanta, I had sworn on the Bible to serve well—just as countless other public servants and leaders, from presidents to police chiefs, had—including Mayor Reed, for that matter. Translated, our oath was, "Cultivating a culture for the glory of God." We each concluded by declaring, "So help me God." If I was ever going to be fired for bringing my faith to work, it should have been the moment I took that oath of office.

In my termination meeting, the city officials had said that my faith influenced the way I led the department. They had meant it as a criticism, but I took it as a compliment. Yes, my faith had shaped the way I championed an "-ism-free" department that had improved the safety of Atlantans.

I didn't cite a chapter and verse for them, but all the leadership principles I taught and modeled were drawn from Scripture. Some of my departmental presentations included quotes from people I named but didn't identify as preachers and Bible teachers, such as "If you want to find a way, you will; if you don't want to (find a way), you will find an excuse."

Like Joseph in Egypt, I hadn't been ashamed to say where my success came from when I was asked. When Pharaoh summoned him to interpret a troubling dream, Joseph made it clear who should get the credit. Genesis 41:16 recounts how he told the king, "It is not in me; God will give Pharaoh a favorable answer." My caution in being too explicit wasn't about being devious but being wise. No one disagreed with the truth of the leadership statements I shared, but I knew some people were so opposed to the Christian faith that they would have dismissed them out of hand if there had been any overt association.

The city continued to spin the story its way as its actions made headlines. Administrators now said I'd been fired not just for failing to seek approval to write the book in advance (false), but also that I'd not remained quiet during my suspension as I had been directed (also false). Plus, they now reasoned, there were concerns my book could spark a lawsuit from someone in the fire department under Title VII of the Civil Rights Act, claiming sexual discrimination because of my views.

In time, the rationale would shift further. A city spokesperson told journalists that the religious nature of the book wasn't the reason I had been let go—which, of course, contradicted Mayor Reed's earlier statement about my views not being in sync with his—but because I had shown poor judgment and not followed work protocols.

Realizing that this was going to be a fight that was beyond my ability to handle alone, I met again with Jonathan Crumly and Garland Hunt, who in turn introduced me to David Cortman and Kevin Theriot from ADF. As these two men spoke about ADF's work representing Christians embroiled in legal issues brought on by standing for their beliefs, I was impressed by their personal faith and their professional expertise. I felt confident that I would be in safe hands with ADF.

A week after I took off my firefighter uniform for the last time, I wore a suit to Georgia's Capitol Rotunda for a rally in my support organized by the Georgia Baptist Mission Board. Hundreds of people crowded in to show they were standing with me. I was moved by the turnout. Later that month, ADF filed a complaint with the Equal Employment Opportunities Commission on the grounds that the city had discriminated against me because of my faith. It was the first round in a legal battle that would stretch on much longer than I anticipated.

If the attendance at the rally was encouraging, so were the letters that started to come in from around the country as news about my termination spread. "Thank you for being a voice in the wilderness!" wrote a woman named April. "It is sad to see how our country has embraced evil as good and good as evil. I'll be praying for you and your family." Eighty-one-year-old Mary thanked me for my stand, saying, "You are one of very few that is showing the true spirit of America."

I began to get a clearer sense that something bigger was going on in the nation in regard to religious liberty, far beyond my dispute with the city of Atlanta, when I went out to ADF's headquarters offices in Arizona for a couple of days of media training. There I met several other Christians from around the country who had found themselves targeted for their faith whom ADF also was representing.

There was Jack Phillips, who had been creating exquisite custom cakes at his Masterpiece Cakeshop in Lakewood, Colorado, since 1993. He was sued after politely declining to make a cake for two men that celebrated their same-sex marriage because it would conflict with his faith.

Blaine Adamson found himself in court after explaining to folks from the Gay and Lesbian Services Organization in Lexington, Kentucky, that his Hands On Originals printing company couldn't provide T-shirts for the group's pride festival because its message contradicted his personal beliefs.

Barronelle Stutzman was taken to court by the Washington attorney general after she told a longtime customer (who was a personal friend) that she could not design custom floral arrangements for his same-sex wedding because of her relationship with Jesus Christ.

ADF advised us all how to handle questions from secular journalists, who were often more liberal than conservative in their worldviews. Our legal team knew that our sort of cases had to be fought in two arenas: before judges, but also in the court of public opinion. I'd had some experience dealing with the press as a fire chief, but I still welcomed additional help in doing so.

What struck me most from our time together in Arizona was what an unlikely group this was. The LGBT lobby was portraying these people as bigots and hatemongers, but all I saw in them was kindness and conviction. These were small-business people who wanted to serve God well by serving their local communities well. There was Jack, always smiling and warm; Blaine, caring and thoughtful; Barronelle, the quintessential white-haired, kind grandmother. They weren't imposing their views on anyone else; they just didn't believe someone else should be able to do that to them. While they were determined to stand their ground, they weren't militant or angry.

One thing that differentiated my case from theirs was my position as a public servant: The high-profile nature of my termination made me something of the public face of religious liberty issues. I didn't particularly enjoy being in the spotlight, but I believed it was a platform God had given me, so I determined to represent Him as well as I could.

■   ■   ■

I began to travel fairly frequently, speaking not only in churches, but also to other religious liberties groups and at conferences. I would share my story, along with five lessons for anyone facing similar challenges or other kinds of suffering. It was always rewarding to have people tell me how I had encouraged them in their circumstances.

Some of those I got to speak with would remark on how cheerful I was, considering the situation I was in. They seemed to expect me to be worn down and weary, or at least worried. I would explain that I was simply living the truth of God's Word. I was doing what we are told to do in Philippians 4:6—praying about concerns instead of being anxious—and experiencing the result promised in the next verse: "And the peace of God, which transcends all understanding, will guard your hearts and your minds in Christ Jesus."

I wasn't just putting on a brave face; I truly did have joy in knowing that God was with me and was using my situation for His purposes. I believe that's what God wants for all believers going through trials. After all, James 4:1 urges, "Consider it pure joy, my brothers and sisters, whenever you face trials of many kinds." Note that this is in the present tense, now, not when it's all over and you can look back with relief. I suspect that when Shadrach, Meshach, and Abednego realized that Jesus was with them in the fiery furnace, they were jumping up and down—and not because they were so hot, but because they were overjoyed by His presence.

The affirmation I received as I traveled confirmed the new path God was opening up for me. I'd had this pregnant feeling for about eighteen months before my suspension. While things were still going well in the AFRD, I had begun to look ahead. With Mayor Reed's second term due to end, I knew a new administration meant I might soon be looking for another job. I would have been Atlanta's fire chief for the best part of ten years by then, anyway; all my leadership experience and training told me that was around the time to make way for someone new.

So I'd had an inkling that something was coming my way. And while firefighting had been my life up to that point, I had been open to letting it go. A headhunting organization had invited me to apply for the position of interior minister in a Muslim nation in the Middle East, unlikely as that sounds. Then, days before I was suspended, I had been approached by Ollie Tyler, the newly elected mayor of Shreveport. She wanted to know whether I might be interested in returning to the city as assistant chief administration officer.

Serving again in my hometown had some appeal, so we talked about what that might look like. We were in the final stage of negotiations when things blew up, after which one of the first calls I made was to Ollie. After talking with her transition team, she told me they had decided it simply wouldn't be good for the new administration to bring in someone with such a cloud hanging over him. I told her I understood.

Now, as I found myself on different platforms talking about the assault on religious liberty, I could see how God had been preparing me for this situation for a long time—disciplining myself to raise my voice as a training officer, teaching in church, speaking to the media as fire chief. All these experiences had been grooming me for the new role I needed to embrace.

I didn't do so lightly, however. Though I had spoken in church many times, from leading Sunday School classes to speaking from the pulpit as fire chief, I had never considered myself to be a preacher, per se. Grandma Meme had always said I was going to grow up to be one when I was a boy, but it had made no sense to me at the time. While I loved church, I dreaded the annual Easter speeches the kids had to make. They were only two or three sentences long, but standing in front of people like that as a boy had terrified me.

I'd worked to overcome that fear of raising my voice as a firefighter, but I still saw preaching as a special responsibility and opportunity beyond my capabilities. God had revealed to me years earlier that I would be in the full-time ministry of church administration at some stage, but I hadn't envisioned that as involving the pulpit. So I had been surprised when, in one of my personal devotional times during my suspension, I had felt God telling me, *I'm calling you to preach the Gospel.* I'd wept at the privilege and the weight of it all.

Caught in the middle of all that was going on, I didn't know what to do with what I sensed. I wrote it down in my journal but kept it to myself. That made things awkward sometime later when Carolyn and I had a visit from Anika, a minister who lived across the street. After taking a seat in our living room, she said to me, "There's something different about you, Kelvin. You've been called to preach, haven't you?"

Because I'd not told Carolyn about what God had spoken to me, I felt caught. I mumbled a denial to Anika, but I felt terrible inside. The unrest kept growing in me until a couple of weeks or so after my firing, when I tossed and turned in bed, unable to sleep. Sometime during the middle of the night, I nudged Carolyn awake.

"Carolyn, God has called me to preach," I told her, bursting into tears. She hugged me. "Kelvin, you just do whatever God has called you to do," she murmured, and I drifted into sweet sleep.

In light of all that, I wasn't entirely surprised when Pastor Oliver invited me to join the staff of Elizabeth Baptist as chief operating officer, overseeing some of the ministries and preaching from time to time. I was humbled and honored, however. In my first message from the pulpit in June 2015, I shared how God had worked in my life to prepare me for this new role—and acknowledged how Anika, who was there to hear me, had been right in discerning God's hand on me.

To some people, going from fire chief to church staff seemed like a sharp right turn, but I saw it as a continuation of God's call on my life. Sometimes we confuse the big picture, which is our calling, with the smaller details, which are divine assignments that can change. For more than three decades, I'd protected and rescued people from the flames in the fire department; I was still doing the same thing, as far as I was concerned, just in a different context. And I still had the title of chief!

■　　■　　■

Meanwhile, my dispute with the city of Atlanta continued. The Equal Employment Opportunity Commission (EEOC) complaint had been a legal placeholder while ADF prepared a fuller case against the city and Mayor Reed. Filed in February 2015, it argued that they had violated my First and Fourteenth Amendment rights on nine counts related to freedom of speech, free exercise of religion, freedom of association, and due process.

Mayor Reed came out swinging. Asked about my lawsuit by Fox 5, one of the local TV stations, he said, "He is going to lose, and in the process his reputation is going to be destroyed because people are going to see that he was dishonest."

The comment hurt, but I knew better than to get into a public argument with the mayor. I bit my tongue and chose to let the legal process play out, confident that I would be vindicated in the end. My assurance was not only in the facts of the matter, but in clear biblical precedent: I knew from studying the Bible that no authority figure had ever taken action against a child of God who was standing for truth and righteousness and won. Think about it: Potiphar versus Joseph; Sanballat versus Nehemiah; Haman versus Mordecai; and Nebuchadnezzar versus Shadrach, Meshach, and Abednego. The list goes on. In light of how all those situations turned out, if anything, what I felt for Mayor Reed was compassion. I remembered Jesus's instructions in the Sermon on the Mount that we should pray for those who persecute us.

With the city dragging its feet in providing relevant documentation of its claims against me, things moved slowly. As lead attorney on my case, Kevin Theriot did a great job of keeping me informed of its progress, but weeks would go by without any real movement. I was encouraged by the ongoing support I received. Of particular note was a letter written to Mayor Reed by Peter Kirsanow, one of the eight members of the U.S. Commission on Civil Rights. He pointed out the irony of the defendants' firing me for writing a book containing what they called in a court filing "moral judgments about certain groups of people," because the very basis of their action was their moral judgment of me.

"Furthermore," he went on,

if knowing that someone holds views with which some people disagree threatens the cohesion of the AFRD, the people of Atlanta may wish to consider hiring some new firefighters. It is hard to imagine that people who wilt upon learning that a book they are under no obligation to read contains statements with which they disagree will have the intestinal fortitude to rush into burning buildings. It seems unlikely that the Atlanta Fire Rescue Department is comprised of such fragile flowers. It is respectfully submitted that this is not a good-faith attempt to maintain morale and cohesion. It is simply a purge of the disfavored at the behest of the politically correct. That is unconstitutional and contrary to American ideals.

■   ■   ■

One indication of the seriousness and significance of my case was being asked to appear before Congress during a hearing in July 2016. I was one of just eight people from both sides of the issue invited to testify before the House Committee on Oversight and Reform regarding the First Amendment Defense Act (FADA). Introduced in the wake of the Supreme Court's ruling the previous year legalizing same-sex marriage nationwide, over-riding many state laws and constitutional amendments defining it as the union of one man and one woman, the bill sought to prohibit the federal government from discriminating against anyone for their sincerely held religious beliefs or moral convictions about marriage.

There was a different tenor to the proceedings than when I'd last been on Capitol Hill for my confirmation hearing as U.S. fire administrator in 2009. I found myself seated between James Obergefell, the plaintiff in the groundbreaking U.S. Supreme Court same-sex marriage decision, and Barney Frank, the longtime Democratic member of the House of Representatives who was the first member of Congress to marry a same-sex partner while in office before his retirement in 2013.

In the few minutes I was given, I told of fulfilling my childhood dream and how my own experiences with prejudice had compelled me to ensure others were protected from similar discrimination.

"My faith does not teach me to discriminate against anyone, but rather it instructs me to love everyone without condition and to recognize their inherent human dignity and worth as being created in the image of God, and to lay down my life if necessary in the service of my community as a firefighter," I said. "In fact, it was because of the discrimination that I myself suffered that I made a promise that under my watch, if I were ever in charge, no one would ever have to go through the horrors of discrimination that I endured."

At the close of my remarks, Frank leaned over and told me, "What they did to you was wrong. That should not have happened."

His opinion was referenced a few weeks later when I returned to the capital to receive the National Religious Broadcasters' annual Faith & Freedom Award. As he presented me with it, NRB President and CEO Jerry A. Johnson said that I had "become a hero not just for protecting our communities, but for standing bravely in the face of what even some extreme liberals like former Representative Barney Frank seem to think is unjust discrimination for his faith."

It wasn't the first time I had been described as a hero for what I had done, but I was growing increasingly uncomfortable with the label. Without diminishing the importance of my case, I didn't think I'd done anything terribly brave. Yes, I had paid a price for my beliefs, but it hardly seemed to be on the same level as the price that Christians in other parts of the world have paid. They didn't just risk losing their job; their very lives were at stake.

The gulf between my experience and that of some other believers seemed only wider to me when I was invited to participate in the World Summit in Defense of Persecuted Christians in May 2017. Organized by the Billy Graham Evangelistic Association, the event brought more than 600 participants from almost 150 countries to Washington, D.C.

I was incredibly moved to hear some of the stories. Men jailed and killed for preaching about Jesus. Women murdered by their own husbands for turning to Christ. Families forced from their homes. What I had been through paled so much in comparison that I felt almost embarrassed to be included in their numbers. But remarkably, some of those overseas believers I had the privilege to spend time with told how me how hearing about my situation had encouraged them. It didn't make a lot of sense to me at first. In light of what they were facing, my case seemed like an inconvenience, at best. No, they assured me—seeing someone in America go through an experience like mine emboldened them to continue to stand firm.

I came away from that event with a renewed awareness of the significance of my case regarding religious liberty. Without the freedom to believe—or not—as we choose, all our other freedoms are jeopardized. If America accepts the notion that the government can control what and when you can believe, then Christians and others in this country will be in danger of losing much more than their jobs.

CHAPTER THIRTEEN

A Crucial Victory

I have come to set the world on fire, and I wish it were already burning!

—Luke 12:49 NLT

Do not be fainthearted or afraid; do not panic or be terrified by them. For the Lord your God is the one who goes with you to fight for you against your enemies to give you victory.

—Deuteronomy 20:3–4

Attorneys for the city and Mayor Reed filed for a summary dismissal of my lawsuit. At a hearing before U.S. District Court Judge Leigh Martin May in October 2015, an attorney for the city argued that I had never been told I couldn't hold the views I had about sexuality, "but he certainly can't bring that mess to City Hall, and that's what he did." In response, Kevin Theriot acknowledged that Mayor Reed had discretion to hire and fire but asserted "that discretion ends when it violates the Constitution of the United States."

When Judge May ruled a few weeks later that I deserved a hearing on five of the nine points ADF had raised—rights under the First and Fourteenth Amendments—the city seemed to change its position, saying the lawsuit was not about religious beliefs or the First Amendment, but over the fact that I had not followed the rules for outside employment. This was quite a shift from Mayor Reed's original statements to the media, which had made it clear I was let go because I had expressed views he disagreed with.

Things went quiet on the legal front for a long time. However, I remained plenty busy. In my new role at Elizabeth Baptist, I helped lead the church through the kind of strategic planning process we had done in the fire departments in Shreveport and Atlanta. In addition, I had been spending a lot of time studying the ways God develops a man. Much like with my time digging into what was really going on with God's question to Adam—"Who told you that you were naked?"—I developed the outline of a teaching series that might one day become a book.

I'd learned this: Just as there are seasons in agriculture, there are seasons in our lives—cultivation, seed time, and harvest. There are periods of preparation—breaking up the ground and making it ready; periods of sowing, watering, weeding, pruning, and tending to ensure the crop develops to its fullest extent; and periods of reaping the benefits and blessings of all the work that has been done. They don't all occur at the same time in the different areas of your life; you may be getting pruned in your career field while harvesting ripe fruit in the pasture of parenting.

In farming, seasons aren't a one-and-done deal. You don't complete just one cycle; the seasons are cyclical. The same is true in our personal lives: we cooperate with God as He shapes us more into the likeness of Jesus. Over time we grow, bearing more fruit of the Spirit—the personality and character of Christ—

through being pruned and nurtured. People who haven't seen me since college should notice something different about me—and not just a little less hair and a little more waist! They should be able to see more of the fruit of the Holy Spirit in my life—more love, joy, peace, patience, kindness, goodness, gentleness, faithfulness, and self-control.

I was reminded of this process during the long months of legal silence. On the second anniversary of my suspension, in December 2016, God brought to mind James 5:7–8, which I recorded in my journal: "Be patient, then, brothers and sisters, until the Lord's coming. See how the farmer waits for the land to yield its valuable crop, patiently waiting for the autumn and spring rains. You too, be patient and stand firm, because the Lord's coming is near."

The next signs of movement came in February 2017, when everyone who had been part of events was deposed for the forthcoming trial. I was interviewed for eight grueling hours by the city's attorneys, who were looking to trip me up somehow. They kept trying to get me to agree that I'd failed to follow Mayor Reed's directions during my suspension—part of their new strategy of making my firing more about procedure than principle. I held my ground, explaining that I had been told not to speak directly to the media and that I had followed that direction. In fact, when a fire service colleague from another state had contacted me to ask how churches there might get behind me, I'd told him that I couldn't get involved in that. But I did point him to the Georgia Baptist Mission Board to find out more.

As part of their due diligence, the city's attorneys had searched my old emails and came across a document from some years previously called "Sex and Righteous Men." It was a collection of notes on the Bible's teaching on sexuality I'd collected for a church course I had taught. The city's attorneys tried to make it seem like this was another example of my being biased against members of the LGBT community. I explained, no—it was just historic biblical teaching on sexuality. I found it noteworthy that in all their searching through my past communications they had not found a single instance where I had spoken negatively about or dealt in a discriminatory way with someone who had different views on sexuality. If some notes about the Bible's teaching on sex was the best they could come up with as evidence of my bias, I felt fairly safe.

Having come through my own cross examination, I chose to sit through the depositions of the city's witnesses. It was difficult at times to hear things being misrepresented without being able to respond. What was most disappointing was what seemed to be the convenient amnesia so many people I'd respected and enjoyed working alongside seemed to experience. One refreshing exception was the fire department's public information officer. During her interview, she made it clear she did not agree with what I had written in my book, but she said she had never seen me treat anyone differently. The way I was being represented was nothing like the person she had worked with, she said.

With depositions taken and appeals for summary judgment on ADF's part and another for summary dismissal by the city, everything seemed to stall once again for a few months. At a hearing with Judge May in November 2017, the city once again tried to misrepresent what I had written in the book. But all I had done was quote Scripture, not express a personal opinion.

■　　■　　■

I was in my office at Elizabeth Baptist on December 20, 2017, when I got a call from Kevin Theriot. "Great news, Kelvin!" he told me. Judge May had delivered her ruling: She agreed that my firing had been unconstitutional. Requiring me to have my message "cleared" before publication violated my rights under the First Amendment. My four other claims against the city and Mayor Reed, including violation of my freedom of speech, had been dismissed.

To be honest, my immediate reaction was muted. It felt more like a defeat than a victory. Kevin tried to encourage me by reminding me of the bigger picture. Part of the legal strategy had been to challenge my firing on every appropriate ground. We only needed to win on one of them. And in doing so we had secured a strong precedent for other Christians in public service: They did not have to leave their faith at home when they went to work, nor get permission to speak about their faith on their own time.

The points the judge had dismissed were a disappointment, Kevin agreed. But they were only a setback, not a final word. Those opinions could be challenged at another time, in another context. The religious liberties war might not have been over, but we had won an important battle. It was time to let someone else take on the next round in the campaign for religious freedom.

What he said made sense, but it didn't entirely lift my spirits. I was under a bit of a cloud for a few days. Studying Judge May's ruling helped me get a clearer perspective. She pointed out inconsistencies in the city's guidelines for approving outside earnings. The rules were "over-inclusive," applying to situations "plainly untethered from the employee's job," she wrote. "This policy would prevent an employee from writing and selling a book on golf or badminton on his own time and, without prior approval, would subject him to firing. It is unclear to the Court how such an outside employment would ever effect the City's ability to function, and the City provides no evidence to justify it."

Judge May concluded that "the potential for stifled speech far outweighs an unsupported assertion of harm." Additionally, she found the city's standards for judging whether something might be harmful to its interests to be too vague. She cited part of the city's guidelines, noting "this does not pass constitutional muster."

There were other positives in the ruling. For instance, Judge May noted that the city had admitted the teachings in *Who Told You That You Were Naked?* were "consistent with the Bible and historic Christian teaching."

All of that was encouraging. However, I was disheartened by her dismissal of my other claims. She seemed to be saying that if you publicly express conservative, historic Christian views about marriage and sexuality, you are not suited for high public office. "The Court could foresee individuals who might contend their fire department response time was not sufficient because of their sexual orientation or otherwise, regardless of the veracity of that claim," she wrote. That was deeply troubling to me. Not only was it absurd in practice—911 operators don't ask a caller for their ethnicity or sexual persuasion—but the principle was disturbing. It meant that a Christian was effectively barred from public service at a senior level simply because someone who didn't share his or her worldview could make an unsubstantiated claim of discrimination.

With an ongoing ethics investigation related to the previous administration, Mayor Reed's successor, Keisha Lance Bottoms, was understandably eager to separate her office from the past. All that was left was to see if we could come to some sort of agreement on the compensation I was due. Par for the course, it took longer than I anticipated.

We met with a mediator in an attorney's office in North Atlanta in October 2018. He talked with the city representatives first and came in with their offer, an unsurprisingly low-ball figure. David Cortman, ADF's senior counsel, who had provided oversight during the whole case, made it clear that number wasn't even worth considering and told the mediator what sum we would entertain. He took that back to the city team and returned in short order with another low figure.

"Look, we're not going to be doing this all day," David said. "This is what we consider to be reasonable, and if they can't agree, we might as well pack up and go home." And we did, having been there for less than an hour.

Failing to reach an agreement left the prospect of a trial to reach a verdict on the damages. Though I knew God had been with me through the previous four years, it had been a draining time. I was not looking forward to another round of legal conflict.

■   ■   ■

One of the dangers of weariness is that it can lead to discouragement. That is why I was so glad that I had developed the practice of regularly journaling about my walk with God. I had something to fall back on—written evidence of times God had spoken to and encouraged me.

I'd always been an avid note-taker. At the fire training academy and then at any conference I attended, I had always written down what I was hearing. The process didn't just help me concentrate on what was being said; it gave me something to refer to and review later. I started to do the same with my thoughts and questions as I began to read the Bible seriously. At first, I'd scribble in any handy notebook, but in time I decided to get journals specifically for my devotional time with God.

Today it's just part of my everyday life. Each morning, I write down insights, observations, and questions about Bible passages I read. I write prayers. I write what I sense God is saying to me as I wait on Him. Doing so helps make it more concrete. It's easy to forget or dismiss a thought or impression later, but when it's written down it somehow has a greater permanence.

For some guys, this is a bit of a stretch; they dismiss it as somehow feminine. But I point out that it's not keeping a diary; it's having a conversation with God. And, I remind them, there's a good biblical precedent: David journaled, and some of his writings continue to inspire us to this day. I'm not saying my words are as important as the Psalms, of course, but I am filled with joy at the thought that one day my grandchildren and their children—and so on—will be able to pick up my journals. I hope they will learn something about me from them, but more importantly, I hope they will learn something about God as they follow my relationship with Him through the different ages and stages of my life. I believe there is something special about their being able to read all that in my own hand, not just in a file I saved to a computer. It is somehow more intimate, more revealing.

Journaling had been the source of my fight with the city of Atlanta. The thoughts I captured about men's struggles with condemnation had been the genesis of *Who Told You That You Were Naked?*. Now these thoughts were the source of encouragement to keep going. While reading back over previous journal entries a few days after the mediation talks broke down, I wrote:

> God understands what I'm going through and He knows why I am going through it. In fact, He is allowing it because He is preparing me for something greater later. The duration of this legal journey is not in the hands of mere men, this journey is under the sovereign supervision of God. It will end in His timing, and it will end in a way that glorifies Him. All my hope is in Jesus. I trust in the husbandry of God. He is preparing me to run with the horses.

All this was on my mind as I drove home one sunny day in early December 2018. *Lord, how long is this going to be?* I wondered. I sensed Him say that I had been through cultivation and seed time in my fight with the city and that harvest was just around the corner. Literally, it turned out.

Just as I rounded a bend toward my house, my cell phone rang: "Chief." It was David Cortman. "We've settled your case for $1.2 million."

"That's great news!" I told him.

A tremendous sense of relief washed over me: It was finally done. I had been vindicated. I had stood my ground, not just for myself but on behalf of others, and God had honored my faithfulness. Sensing His presence and affirmation through it all had been reward enough, but the money was a nice bonus, for sure.

Hearing the amount of the award announced on the news later that day came as a surprise. David had told me the city had wanted to keep the details of the settlement private, which was fine by me. But now it was public knowledge, apparently disclosed by the city. Was this a last shot at me, an attempt to make me look bad somehow, as though I was making a money grab?

Certainly, I wasn't entirely comfortable having that detail out there. There are some things about our lives that are personal and private. It wasn't that I was embarrassed, but I didn't want people to get the impression that I had hit some sort of jackpot. A million-plus dollars (before tax) is no small sum, of course, but my firing had cost me years of a fire chief's salary. Plus, what price do you put on your reputation? For all that I had tried to do to ensure no one ever endured any kind of prejudice under my leadership, I would forever be known by people who only googled my name as the fire chief fired for being a bigot.

When the money came through just after Christmas, I banked it and went to Elizabeth Baptist. I told the lady in the finance department, "I don't want to wait until Sunday to pay my tithe," and wrote out a big six-figure check. All of a sudden,

I was overwhelmed with emotions. I wept tears of joy and gratitude.

See, the settlement hadn't just signaled the end of four years of facing the fire. It had also been the fulfillment of a longtime hope, another example of how God weaves the different strands of our lives together in a way we often cannot imagine.

Corrie ten Boom, the famous Dutch evangelist, sometimes took a piece of embroidery with her when she spoke. She would show the back side with all its seemingly random lines of thread, and talk about how often life seems like that, as though it makes no sense. But then she would talk about how God was using all those different situations and events and challenges to create a work of art out of our lives—and then she would turn the cloth over to reveal a beautifully embroidered crown on the other side.

In my case, one of those threads went back seven years, during my first turn as fire chief in Atlanta. I'd been listening to a teaching by a Christian financial planner that had made a big impression on me. He talked about how God did not intend for His children to be in debt all their lives. Everyone should have a debt-free date in mind, he suggested, when they would own everything free and clear, owing nothing. They should work and budget and plan toward that day.

I had always tried to practice wise financial stewardship, and this teacher's advice made a lot of sense to me. As I thought about what he said and reviewed my own situation, I grabbed a piece of paper from a notepad on my desk and scribbled down my debt-free date, which I pinned to my noticeboard. This was in November 2011, and the date I wrote on the piece of paper: End of 2018, just as it turned out. We were debt-free!

Though it was all finally over, it took some time for that reality to really sink in. Having carried the weight of waiting for so long, it wasn't until three or four months later that I really sensed it had lifted. One morning, I woke up with a lightness I hadn't realized had been missing. It was not that I had been depressed during the long legal process—I'd been so aware of God's presence and confident of His deliverance—but there had always been a sense of being on the alert for what was next, like waiting for a call-out at the fire station.

Packing up all the case files I'd collected over the years and putting them away in storage closed the door on that extended chapter, freeing me up for what God had next.

CHAPTER FOURTEEN

Forgiving and Facing Forward

*And the princes, governors, and captains, and the
king's counsellors, being gathered together, saw these
men, upon whose bodies the fire had no power, nor was
an hair of their head singed, neither were their coats
changed, nor the smell of fire had passed on them.
Then Nebuchadnezzar spake, and said, Blessed be the
God of Shadrach, Meshach, and Abednego, who hath
sent his angel, and delivered his servants that trusted
in him, and have changed the king's word, and yielded
their bodies, that they might not serve nor worship any
god, except their God.*

—*Daniel 3:27–28 KJV*

I have so much to be thankful for and so many people to be
grateful to. I credit my legal victory to the great skill of Kevin
and David and the rest of the ADF team and to the prayers of so
many people not only across the United States, but around the
world. This great team of intercessors was mobilized by so many
media and ministry leaders and organizations that championed
my case—among them Eric Metaxas, Todd Starnes, Dr. James
Dobson's *Family Talk*, DayStar Television, the Family Policy

Council, the Billy Graham Evangelistic Association, the Southern Baptist Convention, the Georgia Baptist Mission Board, and Pastor Oliver and the members of Elizabeth Baptist. I owe them all so much.

I won't pretend it wasn't satisfying to be exonerated. I may not have won on all the points in my lawsuit, but the evidence presented made it absolutely clear that I had never discriminated against anyone. Despite a thorough effort, the city had been unable to come up with a single concrete instance that would have been enough to justify its actions. Contrary to what Mayor Reed had predicted, if anything the whole process had cemented my reputation as someone who was fair and unbiased.

To a degree, that was important personally. It's not pleasant to be unfairly accused. But mostly it was important in defending a matter of principle—that expressing biblical views on marriage and sexuality does not require permission from the government.

Despite my quiet satisfaction, I made a point to celebrate my victory publicly only in a way that honored God and glorified Him. It's one thing to win a tough boxing match on points and appreciate the moment when your hand is thrust high in the air as the winner by the referee, but it's another to taunt the opponent you just defeated. We need to leave the consequences to God. The Apostle Paul made that very clear when he wrote, "Do not take revenge, my dear friends, but leave room for God's wrath, for it is written: 'It is mine to avenge; I will repay,' says the Lord" (Romans 12:19). He was referring to the time God told the Jews through Moses, "It is mine to avenge; I will repay.

In due time their foot will slip; their day of disaster is near and their doom rushes upon them" (Deuteronomy 32:35).

In fact, God is so determined that we have a good attitude toward those who wrong us that He will actually lighten up on wrongdoers if we take too much pleasure in their defeat. Proverbs 24:17–18 says, "Do not gloat when your enemy falls; when they stumble, do not let your heart rejoice, or the Lord will see and disapprove and turn his wrath away from them."

I decided I was not going to spend too much time worrying and wondering about Mayor Reed. I had too much else that needed my focus. However, I couldn't fail to see news reports that tracked how his time as mayor ended on more of a rather low note, with a corruption scandal involving several aides and contractors. While he denied any wrongdoing and has not been charged with any crimes, the investigation has tarnished the legacy of the man for whom at one time the *Atlanta Journal-Constitution* said, "further greatness beckoned."

Some have speculated that Mayor Reed didn't expect things to blow up the way they did—that he thought suspending me for a month would make enough of a statement to the influential LGBT community, only to find himself having to double down when the Christian community responded so strongly to his actions. I don't know about that; for my part, I simply remain grateful to him for giving me the opportunity to return to and serve a city I love and to be part of strengthening the fire department. And I continue to pray for him, from time to time, as Jesus taught.

It has been satisfying to see how the price many people thought I would pay for my stand has been more than overturned. My reputation is largely intact. I lost a few speaking engagements to fire service groups in the wake of my termination, but I received many more church invitations instead. I lost a few fire service friends, but I gained a whole lot more in churches across the country. And the controversy gave my self-published book a platform I never could have imagined. Rather than silence the message of *Who Told You That You Were Naked?*, my case promoted it: to date I have sold around thirty thousand copies, many more than I ever could have imagined—and an answer to prayer.

Another blessing from it all has been the further deepening of my relationship with Carolyn. Not only did she stand by me and offer support and encouragement through the long legal process, but as the wife of a public figure she faced her own rejection and relationship challenges, doing so with grace and kindness. Her quiet strength only deepened a conviction I have long held: that the second most important decision a man will ever make, after accepting Jesus as his Lord and Savior, is who to ask to be his wife.

It has also been gratifying to learn how the ruling in my case has already had a ripple effect; it has been cited in other cases and legal writings that have defended Christians' rights in the public square. I believe it will protect Bible-believing government workers for many years to come. So, in some ways, I am grateful for all that happened—though I would not have chosen it ahead of time if I had known what was coming.

However, I have needed to be intentional about forgiveness. It isn't always easy, but it is always best. Some people hold on to grudges against others because they think they are somehow getting even with them, but in reality, they are only hurting themselves. As the saying goes, harboring unforgiveness is like drinking poison and hoping the other person will die. It doesn't work like that.

Being black in America gives you lots of opportunities to practice forgiveness. That has certainly been my experience, from the prejudice I first became aware of at Linwood Junior High to the racism I faced upon joining the Shreveport Fire Department. I believe that choosing to let go of grievances and not hold on to hurts kept my heart soft from my formative years on and made it easier for me to hear God.

Then there's the fact that I know only too well how much I have needed God's forgiveness in the past and continue to need it until this day. With His help I have put behind me those sinful ways that kept me from being all I was called to be, and I believe that I am a better person now than I was. That's not being boastful—at least about me. If anything, it's being boastful about God, because He promises that as we pursue Him, He will make us more like Jesus.

Christians should be able to say that they are better than they used to be; it's evidence that they are growing in Christ. If not, something's wrong! They should also be able to see some signs of His goodness in their lives. I'm not talking about the prosperity gospel. But you simply can't spend time with God without becoming more like Jesus and increasing in evidence of His blessing. Yes, His goodness extends to everyone to some degree, but "he rewards those who earnestly seek him" (Hebrews 11:6).

I am not pretending to be perfect. I still have my struggles and issues, and from time to time I find myself having to rise above a feeling of condemnation, just as I wrote about in *Who*

Told You That You Were Naked?. There is plenty in my past for me to be ashamed of, but I know I have been completely and utterly forgiven by God. The double jeopardy clause in the Fifth Amendment says that someone can't be tried twice for the same crime—and the Bible does too. Romans 8:33–34 declares, "Who will bring any charge against those whom God has chosen? It is God who justifies. Who then is the one who condemns? No one."

When I became fire chief in Shreveport, I had the opportunity to retaliate, to pay back some of those who had mistreated me in the past, but I didn't want to go there. Actually, most of the people I'd ever had any issues with ended up becoming friends, to different degrees. Our strong bond forged in the fire service overcame any other differences there may have been. I held no animosity toward anyone. And although I was disappointed by the way Mayor Reed and some of my former colleagues in the city of Atlanta treated me, I never held a grudge against them. In fact, I hope that one day I may cross paths with Kasim Reed again and have an opportunity to shake his hand.

■   ■   ■

My fight with the city of Atlanta may be over, but the bigger cultural conflict isn't. If anything, it is intensifying. In part, that's because of the way the Church has responded—or, more accurately, failed to respond. In many places she has remained silent, not wanting to seem critical. But failing to challenge liberal ideologies and moral relativism has only given them more room in which to flourish. Silence has been taken for passivity and approval. What was once widely recognized as immoral is now celebrated. As Psalm 12:8 says, "The wicked...freely strut about when what is vile is honored by the human race." I believe it's time for the Church to take more of a stand.

This isn't about being hateful; it's actually about being loving. It is not loving to withhold the truth from people for fear that they will persecute you. One of the challenges is that while we think we are speaking the same language as people who disagree with us, we are actually using different dictionaries. For instance, the dictionary that Christians use—the Bible—says that God is love. That's not the same dictionary some members of the LGBT community use. They also talk about "tolerance" differently. To them, it means you can think and believe what you like as long as it lines up with what they think and believe. When you don't, you are being "hateful." But true tolerance is a two-way street. I believe that members of the LGBT community should be free to believe what they do and live the way they choose—and the same for Christians. We can disagree but still live peaceably with each other.

Believing what the Bible teaches about human sexuality is not a license to hate. The Scriptures that declare sex to be God's amazing gift for a man and a woman in marriage also call us to love all people and pray for our enemies. At the end of the day, we can't allow ourselves to be silenced by the fear that we will be misunderstood or misrepresented. We need to spend less time worrying about the allegations others make against us and more time focused on the evidence we provide them—living in a way that demonstrates love, not hate. People said my book showed that I was biased against LGBT folks, but they couldn't point to a single actual instance where I acted in such a way.

I'm not suggesting we go around looking to get into arguments with people, but we must be ready and willing to respond when they state a position that is contrary to God's Word. We can do so kindly and calmly, without getting all hot and bothered. Hopefully they may hear the compassion and care in our voices, even if they don't accept our words.

While we don't set out to be offensive, we also need to remember that the Gospel is unavoidably offensive—it calls sinners to repentance. In Galatians 5:11, the Apostle Paul writes about "the offense of the cross." Much as I am concerned about not offending people unnecessarily, I am more concerned about not offending Jesus by failing to stand for His truth and righteousness.

Recently, I received an email at Elizabeth Baptist from a same-sex couple. They said they'd been attending for a while, loved the worship service, and had a son who enjoyed the youth program. They were thinking about joining the church and wanted to know where we stood on same-sex marriage; would they be accepted?

I didn't send them a list of Bible verses about homosexuality. I told them that I was so glad they'd felt welcome at the church and that we accepted all people. The decision to become members was theirs to make, I went on. I listed the core values we embraced as a church—Bible-based teaching, repentance and salvation, and so on—and said that if they embraced these, then Elizabeth Baptist could be a great home for them. Sadly, I didn't hear from them again; they must have decided that we were not a fit because of our biblically based teaching. But the point was that I did not turn them away; they chose not to pursue membership.

Not all situations are so simple. Another time we had a same-sex couple ask about having their baby dedicated, prompting some real soul-searching and Bible study on the part of the church leadership. Wasn't this a non-issue, because it was really about the baby? In some ways, yes, but what message were we sending to the congregation by bringing a same-sex couple to the front of the church and effectively affirming their lifestyle? Okay, but what about single young moms who wanted to bring their babies for dedication? Well, through the discipleship process in the church, they would have acknowledged turning from their former lifestyle, unlike the same-sex couple. In the end, we decided we could not accommodate the couple's dedication request; we accepted them, but we could not affirm all of their choices.

These are not easy pastoral decisions. They need to be made and communicated as lovingly as possible, anchored in the truths of God's Word.

■   ■   ■

Another reason the Church has failed to stem our cultural landslide is that we have not been united enough. We have been too passive, leaving the work of standing against the tide to a select few. Yet no matter how large or influential one Christian denomination, ministry, or organization might be, it does not have the necessary resources to fight on all the fronts in the war being waged against the Gospel and biblical truths. It's time for the Church to rise to a new level of unity across longstanding denominational, racial, geographical, and political divisions.

I believe that this is possible because of what I experienced during my own trial. As I traveled to churches across the country, I saw the unity of the body of Christ in a new way. I developed more friendships with believers of other ethnicities than I ever had before. Many of the churches that welcomed me with open arms and encouraged me were predominantly white. The out-pouring of love I experienced—people praying for and weeping with me—was profoundly moving. Color wasn't an issue; they stood with me as a brother in Christ.

Each time I got to tell my story, my own faith was renewed. During the long months when not much seemed to be happening, I was reminded of what God had done up to that point and that He was working even when I could not see any evidence of it. However, at one stage a couple of years into the legal dispute, I wondered if I should change my message, maybe speak about something else. I sensed God telling me, *Noah had a three-word sermon for almost one hundred years: It's gonna rain.* So I kept to my same message.

With my own dispute behind me, I continue to travel and share my story as both a warning and an encouragement. It's been helpful not only to those facing some sort of persecution for their faith, but to others just going through some sort of dif-ficulty in life, reminding them that God has purposes in our circumstances we may not yet see. Many times, people thank me for taking the stand I did and wonder whether they will have what it takes to do the same thing if they ever need to. I tell them there are five signs they are ready:

1. When you spend more time rejoicing about what God is doing than complaining about what your enemies are doing. Whatever they are up to cannot thwart the purposes of God: He is going to build

His Church, and the gates of Hell will not prevail against it (Matthew 16:18).

2. When you have more faith in what God can do than fear of what your enemies can do. Faith and fear cannot coexist; as we focus on how great God is, His perfect love drives out fear (1 John 4:18).

3. When you are more pumped by the promises that God has made than you are paralyzed by the threats of your enemies. He is not impressed by them; God laughs at the wicked because He knows their day is coming (Psalm 37:13).

4. When you are more empowered by the words God is speaking than anxious about those your enemies are speaking. They may have a lot to say, but God has the final word; pride goes before a fall (Proverbs 16:18).

5. When you acknowledge the omnipotent authority of the Most High God above and over the limited influence and power of your enemies. They have some power, but He has all power (Matthew 28:18).

■　　■　　■

We are living in a time when too many preachers are taking their cues from politicians, rather than the other way around. Afraid to declare "thus says the Lord," they are tickling itching ears rather than speaking the truth. As a result, political leaders with high approval ratings and national prominence are influencing the people of God on matters that are not aligned with His Word. Elected officials are directing the actions of pastors and preachers according to the agenda of their political party, as opposed to pastors and preachers serving as prophetic guides or counselors to elected officials.

In biblical history, whenever national leaders honored the guidance of the word of God spoken through the patriarchs and prophets, the nation—from the king to the people—prospered. During the times when leaders were prideful and arrogant and rejected the word of God spoken by the patriarchs and prophets, they and the nation suffered famine and calamity.

Thankfully, there are many biblical accounts of patriarchs and prophets who had a resolve of "no compromise" when they interacted with political figures: Abraham, Isaac, Jacob, Moses, Joshua, Samuel, Nathan, and more. There are also accounts of appointed government officials who served under political leaders with the same "no compromise" determination: Joseph, Nehemiah, Shadrach, Meshach, Abednego, Daniel, and others.

There is a sobering example of how things can play out when people have divided loyalties in 1 Kings 18. It involves King Ahab, the political leader of Israel; Obadiah, King Ahab's chief of staff; and Elijah the prophet, the pastor of the congregation of Israel.

The country had suffered under Ahab's rule. He had married Jezebel, who led him away from God to worship Baal. As a result, there was a nationwide drought for three years. Ahab sent Obadiah off to search for water and grass, and who should Obadiah bump into but Elijah, who was on his way to tell the king that rain was coming. When Elijah asked Obadiah to tell Ahab he wanted to meet with him, Obadiah refused. He was afraid the king would kill him.

Rather than do what Elijah, the man of God, said, Obadiah wanted to keep on the right side of Ahab. Now, Obadiah wasn't a total washout. He "feared the Lord greatly," according to 1 Kings 18:3. He had hidden one hundred prophets in caves, providing them with meat and bread. But he feared even more the worldly consequences of standing on God's behalf. In his mind, that would be political suicide. He wanted to remain politically correct.

Too many Christian leaders are the same way today—afraid to deliver a message to a council member, a mayor, a governor, or the president because they don't want to give the impression that they oppose their public-policy positions. They want to stay in the good graces of the political leader rather than on the good side of God.

Obadiah told Elijah how he had hidden and fed the prophets, as though that action was worthy of praise. But he had simply empowered their cowardly dysfunction. One hundred preachers are of no value to God when they're hiding in caves, their voices silenced by fear of political consequences.

For his part, Elijah had a resolve of "no compromise." He boldly went to meet Ahab, even though he knew the king was not happy with him. He followed God's instructions and guidance as His messenger. He had greater faith in the Kingdom consequences than fear of the worldly consequences Ahab had the authority to impose.

Elijah boldly challenged the culture of Baal worship, taking on 850 prophets at Mount Carmel. Even though he knew

Obadiah had hidden 100 prophets, Elijah declared himself to be "the only one of the Lord's prophets left" (1 Kings 18:22). How and why was that? Because no matter how many there may be, prophets are no good when they are hiding in caves! Elijah was more concerned about being biblically correct than politically correct. He was willing to risk political suicide in order to stay on God's side.

That's the challenge for each of us. Are we willing to stand for God against seemingly overwhelming opposition, even when everyone else is in hiding?

I spent most of my working life keeping people safe from fire, reducing its likelihood, and minimizing its impact. But there is one kind of fire I long to see—the kind that engulfed the altar Elijah had doused with water. When Elijah cried out to God and fire from Heaven fell, consuming the altar and all that was on it, everyone who saw it fell on their faces and cried, "The Lord, he is God; the Lord, he is God" (1 Kings 18:39).

When we stand for God, others get to see Him. This wasn't just true for Elijah. Remember Shadrach, Meshach, and Abednego, when King Nebuchadnezzar had them thrown into the fiery furnace for refusing to worship his idol? Those watching were amazed when they looked into the flames and saw a fourth figure. In the words of the popular Hillsong UNITED song, "there was another in the fire."

May that hope and promise strengthen and encourage you when you are facing the fire, knowing that God has long been preparing you for just such a time, that He has been at work in and through all you have experienced in your life—for your ultimate good and for His glory.

Further Information

My own time facing the flames is over, but I continue to encourage and equip others who are facing persecution for their faith. You can find out more about my writing and speaking engagements, as well as other ministry activities, at www. kelvincochran.org/wp/. Speaking invitations and inquiries should be made at https://legacy-management.com/inquiry/ speaker-request/?aq5pg=KelvinCochran.

Additionally, you can learn more about the important work of Alliance Defending Freedom at www.adflegal.org.

Who Told You That You Were Naked? (3G Publishing, Inc.) is available in digital and print editions online or at all good booksellers.

Acknowledgments

Facing the Fire was a project I was compelled to capture in a book, but in some ways it was written by many people whom God sovereignly seeded into my life. I have been blessed to grow among many I affectionately would categorize as trees: family members, church members, friends, and professional colleagues.

I thank God for my mother, Jane Cochran, the most brilliant tree in my life, who raised a grove in my brothers and sisters. Our Christian upbringing and the challenges we endured growing up instilled in me a vision of God and hope in greater possibilities. Were it not for our relationships, I would not know how to love and get along with other people.

I have often said that a man cannot reach his full potential without a wife. While that may not apply to men who have a calling to be single, it is certainly true of me. I am the man I am today because of Jesus Christ and the fruitful vine of Carolyn Marshall. She has been the woman I need to be the man God created me to be. Our journey of holy matrimony has endured the test of time and has produced wonderful olive plants: Tiffane, Kelton, Camille, and our granddaughter, Thailynn.

I have been blessed with two giant oak trees in my life, dynamic pastors who fueled my faith. Most of my spiritual life was shaped by Galilee Baptist Church, where I accepted Christ and was baptized under Dr. E. Edward Jones Sr. Pastor Jones laid a foundation for faith and righteousness and inspired me to biblical manhood and leadership. Dr. Craig L. Oliver Sr. of Elizabeth Baptist Church became my second pastor upon moving to Atlanta, Georgia. His leadership and teaching accelerated my spiritual growth and strengthened me through the most challenging times of my life and calling.

I am grateful to towering redwood trees like Mayors Keith Hightower, Cedric Glover, Shirley Franklin, and Kasim Reed for giving me the opportunity to serve as fire chief. I am grateful to President Barack Obama for appointing me to serve as the United States fire administrator. And I am super-grateful to Fire Chief Dallas W. Greene Jr. for making my childhood dream come true in first hiring me as a Shreveport firefighter.

I could not have made it through the fiery trial of my termination without palm trees like Ed Setzler, Jonathan Crumly, Garland Hunt, and Mike Griffin, through whom I was introduced to the leadership of the Georgia Baptist Mission Board and Alliance Defending Freedom. I thank God for Alan Sears, Mike Farris, Kevin Theriot, David Cortman, and the team of

ADF attorneys and staff that supported me and my family. I was also encouraged by the many ADF clients who shared similar experiences of being persecuted for living out their faith in their business.

Upon being terminated, I received hundreds of cards, calls, emails, and Facebook messages of prayers and inspiration that strengthened and encouraged me on the journey. There are many other friends and colleagues who encouraged me that are too numerous to mention by name.

Finally, I want to express gratitude to D. J. Snell, Andy Butcher, and ADF for supporting me through the writing of this project. I pray that every word in it has been inspired by the Holy Spirit and that God will use this book to encourage believers to stand for truth all over the world.